THE ONES THAT MADE THEIR MARK

THE ONES THAT MADE THEIR MARK

A COLLECTION OF POETRY

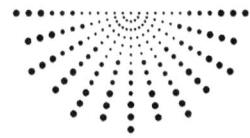

JULIE LAMB

PENNINGTON PRESS

Copyright © 2022 by Julie Lamb

All rights reserved.

No part of this book may be reproduced in any form or by any electronic or mechanical means, including information storage and retrieval systems, without written permission from the author, except for the use of brief quotations in a book review.

Book Cover Design by Erin McWilliams

ISBN: 978-1-948374-82-8

Pennington Press

Goshen, Kentucky 40026

DEDICATION

FOR NELLY SPITZER, A COURAGEOUS WOMAN WHO TAUGHT ME THE WORLD THROUGH HER SAPPHIRE EYES. (*I PROMISED YOU I'D ONE DAY WRITE A BOOK AND DEDICATE IT TO YOU. THIS WAS ALWAYS MEANT FOR YOU, NENY. YOU LEFT ME BEHIND YOUR BEAUTIFUL MARK AND YOUR SWEET TOOTH; I TREASURE BOTH.*)

FOR RACHEL CUMMINS, A BUBBLY RAY OF SUNSHINE WHO CHANGED MY WORLD THROUGH HER GIANT HEART. (*THANK YOU FOR BEING OUR ANGEL ON EARTH. THESE ARE THE ADVENTURES I WOULD HAVE TOLD YOU OVER SUSHI! YOU TURNED MY UNIVERSE LEGENDARY.*)

CONTENTS

Acknowledgments   xi
Foreword   xvii

Prelude   1
  Traffic light   2
Chapter 1: Under the Love of Roots   4
  Limited edition   5
  I'll tell you a secret...   9
  I promise tomorrow I'll be zen   11
  The first friend I made   14
  Even in second grade   21
  Polished   23
  Airports and tabasco dreams   29
  My fake taxi name is Riva   37
  Buy the dress covered in rose petals   45
  Dear Wonder Love of My Life   53
  May your love grow flying   69
  A narrator's fair warning   71
  Insurrection   73
  The Broken Plates   74
  Sketching Tales   77
  I Understand Deep Love Has Legs   81
  She said 'You can pay us after it's over'   85
  Auld Lang Syne   86
  Oh Bless Your Kangaroo Heart   88
  Finding the Circle   94
Chapter 2: The Lust Before Lightning   99
  We run our hands across the continents   100
  Checkmate: The Sea-of-Flames Prom King   103
  Fire and Sugar- and There Was You   107
  The last thought I spill on you   112
  Set a Match   115

Flirting 88 days 'round the sun	117
I like to call him '007	120
Letter to my 13 year-old self	124
Yogurt	130
I'm not your China doll	138
I love a good red flag	141
Try saying no in Italian	145
Desert Atlantis	148
Air Heart	151
Peter Pan Tasted Like Jazz	155
Before You Shouted "Fire!!!" in Heidelberg	161
Whenever I drink	200
To my whiskey lover years ago	202
The Lionheart Buried in the Marshlands	207
What happens to love at first sound?	212
A pep talk to myself in the mirror	221
Chapter 3: Inside the Hive of a Cockroach	233
The day I took off my glasses	234
There's No Room Service in Hell	237
An Ode to the Cockroach Bastard	239
The 72 Secrets You Pushed on Me	241
Acid reflux on Yom Kippur	264
Not Your Julia Roberts	268
First blooms after winter	271
Chapter 4: The Hope in Purple Darkness	275
Fear Can Shine Like Pearls	276
Before Wings Rise	277
Singing Blue Gatorade	279
My father taught me to kick ass and take names	285
Learning to Save a Frog	296
It's a Party	300
Part I	301
The Spiderweb Ally	302
Part II	309
This is The Land of Quarantine:	310
Aquamarine Ablaze	315
An Ode to the Optimists	319
Coffee in my clouds	321

Exploding into a vortex of constellation dreams	324
For Rachel Over the Rainbow	326
Wisdom Can Turn Us to Chicken	335
Apparently Lucy is a Democrat	336
Wanderlust at the Wishing Bridge	340
Dancing words	343
I found myself in a reflector Red Sea	344
Feeling a watermelon solar eclipse	347
He Wore a Hoodie That Said Auschwitz	350
Temporarily Out of Order	351
Call Me Phoenix	355
Extraction	358
Threshold No. 5	359
Epilogue to 2018: I see in gospel truth	361
Allegory of the Cave	367
A world inside my own damn head	369
Time's Smile with Wrinkles	375
...like I'm no longer scared of the dark	378
Snap, Crackle, Pop: It's a Phoenix Kingdom Now	383
About the Author	385

ACKNOWLEDGMENTS

A first collection tapestry sewn with heart patches, stitched with golden seams of soul, doesn't combust out of thin air, like some spectacular Big Bang gone firework-ringing in the galaxy. A book like this begins with a grateful heart, glowing with the lanterns of supporters who lit up this dreamy path forward, ruby torch-alive.

I'd like to thank my family, my first inspirations and mirrors in this world, who let me love them with all the parts that I am for all the parts that they are. This book would not be possible had my father, Doug Lamb, not placed a giant dictionary in our kitchen, teaching me to get excited about all that I didn't know, like it was every new word's birthday, and we had the delight to take a moment and relish every syllable. Thank you, Daddy, for instilling in me a revered magic for the way language can trumpet, and for understanding the way my mind can leap in flowers.

Who I am as a writer would not be possible were it not for my mother's unwavering support, her beacon of love and devotion that has shaped every word that rattled out of my heart with her blazing sincerity within me, a beating heart shaking Spanish hips. Thank you, Mama Lamb, Pat-ty, my endless champion; my Lorelai Gilmore. Your ability to listen, see, reassure, and illuminate is extraordinary.

I'd like to thank my brother, Paul Lamb, my favorite

opposite, who has given me a great deal to look up to since before I could craft my first words. I'm so glad Mom and Dad gave me this life to share with you, even when we're cities and countries apart. I love you, Naomi, Simonsito, and Emito, fully and forever.

This collection of dreams, worlds, stories, and truths especially would not be possible without my cherished mentors. I'd like to sing out a special thank you to Dick Wilson, for making my homecoming to Louisville, Kentucky spring wide-open with the wonder of kindred humans and opportunities. You are a masterful matchmaker who helped me stage a comeback that feels tall, full, and joyful, and I'll forever be humming my gratitude for all you've done for me. Because of you, I work for an agency young Julie went off to seek out in the world, dreaming to find, and I found my own slice of marvelous happiness right in my bourbon-spiced hometown.

This book would have never grown dancing legs, to stand real and honest in this universe, were it not for Dick Wilson's introduction to genius sculptor of poetry in motion, Lee Pennington: an esteemed guide within our special wrinkle in time, whose twinkling wisdom and blessed friendship gave me the courage to let my voice twirl out phoenix-high from a new poet's shy lungs. You told me in our second phone conversation, after you read the first poem I ever sent you, 'Air Heart,' to remember that day- that that was the day I would know I'd one day really have a whole heart's pages inside a book. You gave my wildest dreams the tremendous flight of possibility- and your trust and safekeeping of my most vulnerable thoughts helped me find my own tunnel up to the moon. Thank you for showing me all I could do!

This book has been brewing for many years, in garlic shapes and onion sizes, left simmering inside a watery pot. My very first mentor, Jen Woods, made me hungry to write poetry from deep in my soul, wild, wondrous, and utterly free. Meeting you, interning at Typecast Publishing, writing on book jackets and hearing authors rumble volcanic voices unlike I'd ever seen written in the air, it all shaped my curious footsteps as a young writer. You gave me a crucial first chance without needing to see my experience- you saw my spirit, and that as Robert Frost would say, well, it made all the difference.

I'd like to thank Taylor Swift, who though I highly doubt will ever wander over into my writer's corner of space and time, has felt like a dear friend who inspired me to ignite confessional courage into each word I wrote. You taught me words kindle guitar strings when they are arched straight from the heart; and so I learned to tug my bow, eyes to the sun.

I'd like to share a meaningful thank you with fierce gratitude for Tony Acree; because if you're reading this, that means Hydra Publications has read my first collection of poetry, and decided to give this passionate poet the chance to share her rawest and realest moments with whoever holds this. All it takes is one moment of trust, belief, and the luck to find someone who resonates with who you are- and if you're reading this, Tony Acree offered me that invaluable elixir every beginning writer hopes to find.

I'd like to say thank you to the unsung heroes who saved my life- from Dr. Olson, who walked into a room with a quiet leather black briefcase, emanating brilliant compassion that would change the course of my life, to Dr. Frankel, who beautifully taught me that as Rumi found, 'This being human is a guest house,' and let's embrace each visitor who takes residence within! To the tireless, caring healers at Serenity Health: you all gifted me quite a miracle. It radiates such light, I feel enchantment in every renewed step I've taken since. Dr. Frank:

you and your office took the unruly electricity thundering upstairs and helped me find the rose glow of looking into the light with grounded clarity. Because of each of your efforts, I've been able to live out my dreams in technicolor; and I'll never forget it.

A special thank you goes out to the best friends a girl could ask to find in this great big gumbo of life, love, and laughter. Before there was a book, there were notebooks whispering in satchels, swinging on chairs at cafes where I'd drink tapugezzers and order the pastries of that day, and send a glimpse to see what my friends would think of my latest firecracker, feisty glimmer, flashing misadventure. Because of you, I felt that my thoughts and experiences mattered; and that is the foundation for words to take shape and breathe like a nice bottle of the good stuff we love most. For those who wound their ways into my stories, I hope you see yourself with all the kinship I feel, and the ways you've given me room to grow, to fly, over and over again, to become a whole of me; however those footsteps change through the juicy seasons.

In the order of which we met, I'd like to thank:

Kimmy and Leah. Your pure friendships were a blessing at such an early age, when the world might have otherwise felt scary or alone; you each gave my heart the freedom to find itself, from childhood through adulthood, and I wouldn't be who I am today without your love. You showed me how precious friends become family.

Erin McW. You're my voice of reason, my heaven-sent gift from our bubbly angel best friend, and my cheesecake companion who lets me indulge in the decadence of living. If you're reading this, it means my best friend got to design my first book cover!!! (The Erin and Julie of our 20's are jumping up and down!) I'll love you even if there comes a day we change inside out; because through it all, your bright connection has been a beloved constant.

Bff, Kinga. I still remember the day we toasted in Louisville to all of our adventures and dreams coming true. If mine came to fruition, it's because I saw the way you fearlessly pursued yours! Thank you for believing in me, always. If I dream in color, it's because I saw the way you dared to paint with style out loud. I hope these stories make you (and our icon, Audrey) fiercely proud. I love you to Pluto and back.

My twin, Liz. Thank goodness our trips to the Land of Milk and Honey changed last minute, so that this universe could bring us together. So many of these poems you saw first, letting me bounce off my earliest thoughts, as I followed where the next revisions might lead me. When I'm battling the shadows, I look to you and remember the stars shimmer like buried treasure through the night.

Dafna and Harriet. We are the three musketeers, and not only have you seen some of these poems, you've lived out some of the toughest moments of these stories alongside me. A girl doesn't make it through the fire without the truest supporters by her side; and this girl knows that and is grateful to see you shining on the other side.

Alina. I can still hear the man eavesdropping on our delectable conversation a table away, as we coined some of the very nicknames that melted into these wild tales. Sometimes the best inspiration comes from sharing a coffee and a sassy train ride with a clever and fabulous friend like you!

Daniela. You taught me to move with courage, strength, and balance. I hope that flies through in the words and worlds that follow!

Claudia. Life led me to you at the most precise time. You witnessed these loves and losses unfold, and because we shared our travels through Tel Aviv together, anything that felt 'ominous' suddenly trailed off that much lighter into the sea; because you were by my side! Bless the universe for bringing your velvet radiance so deeply into my life.

To those I've yet to mention: if you've ever shown me loving kindness, genuine support, or offered me a moment in time you felt utterly, completely *you*, I know you've transformed the poet I've gotten to be; and I carry you with me.

To the loves who shattered my heart, the friends whose stars have aligned on different rhythms of the grid, the ghosts, the monsters, and the cherished souls in between: our conversations, our frustrations and flights, the moments we've drunk together and the blood we've spilled apart into the rolling seas; you are the ones that have made your mark. For better and for worse, I hold my hands in prayer up to the universe, thankful for the wonders and wild-seekers who have made me, through shapes, through stories, through seafoam and sugar, through sadness and scintillating sizzle, through the sudden and the still.

To Kentucky, you galloped through my veins and wherever I roamed, you bubbled inside me, singing me home.

To Israel, you brought pieces of me to life in ways I never dreamed could happen. Your enchantment lingers in the ways I stride the earth, long after I've moved map miles apart.

To you, the reader: I thank you for the bond we're about to share. If you're taking time to read what I've dared to witness on paper, you'll never know just how much you mean to me.

Thank you all, with love, light, and lilting magic,

-J

FOREWORD

JULIE LAMB: AN AMAZING NEW POET

Over a year ago, my friend, Dick Wilson, called me and asked if I would mentor Julie Lamb, a writer friend of his. Dick told me that Julie had recently returned from Israel where she had spent the past three years, and he was really impressed with her creative energy and her writing.

I said I would be happy to, and Dick set up a three-way telephone conversation between all of us. We spoke for about fifteen minutes or so and exchanged emails, phone numbers and Facebook connections.

It was obvious with the Covid-19 pandemic spreading and the lockdown already in place, the regular method of mentoring, that is, setting up face-to-face meetings every so often to discuss the mentee's writing, simply was not going to work. We would have to do everything over the internet.

At first I was somewhat leery of the internet idea (never having tried such a thing before), and I was not sure how

FOREWORD

successful our mentor-mentee experience would be. Julie and I, however, settled into a routine of her sending me a poem, usually one or more a week, and within a few days I would respond back to her; then she would respond to me and send me new poems.

Immediately after Julie sent me her first poem and my reading it, I knew I was working with a very gifted and very talented writer. I was enormously excited with what she was able to do with words, how she handled them, and the overall impact of her poems. Every new poem she sent throughout the year of our working together simply confirmed my first impression.

She already had a book idea in mind from the outset, and with each new submission, she told me where she perceived that particular poem would fit into her book.

We had been working our digital magic for eight months when Dick Wilson suggested that Julie and I should meet. So we set up a backyard pandemic style visit with Jill Baker, Julie, Dick, and me in our full Lone Ranger disguises, all the time keeping our WHO-suggested social distances.

So on October 4, 2020, I met Julie for the first time. We got to know each other a little bit better.

On my birthday, seven months later, on May 1, 2021, I got to see Julie the second time as she and her father stopped by and joined in my backyard 82nd birthday celebration. Since we all were vaccinated against the pandemic, and we were in the yard, we could actually see each other sans masks—a real treat, since our pandemic world had changed the way we met and greeted each other, if at all.

Then on May 23, 2021, Julie and I met in an actual face-to-face meeting, our very first mentor-mentee meeting, and Julie handed me a copy of her first book manuscript—*The Ones That Made Their Mark*. Most of the poems I had seen throughout the

FOREWORD

past year, but Julie had added several new ones and I went over those with her.

We were both extremely excited. This was the culmination of a great journey we had taken during this pandemic-altered world for more than a year now. I had told Julie earlier, after first seeing her poetry, that when she got her book finished, I wanted to be the one to introduce her to the world, and here I was, holding her book manuscript in my hand.

Well, world, here she is! I hope you find her work as exciting as I find it. I hope you are equally moved by her words as I am. Here she is fresh as rain, bright as morning sun, timeless as stars dancing across the universe.

Please welcome her.

I have a strong feeling you are going to be seeing a great deal more of Julie. For anyone with her talent and her gift of words, silence is simply not an option.

--Lee Pennington
Louisville, Kentucky
June, 2021

PRELUDE

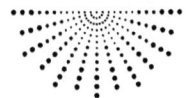

TRAFFIC LIGHT

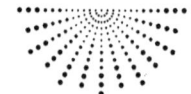

My feelings rattle color
like the sky shifting through sunset
I beseech you
pause for danger and *beware-*
my dearest compasses
my loved ones
my gasoline-snapping foes
enter here at your own
beautiful, disastrous, heart-whistling risk:
These are the love-dipped chapters
I spilled my soul's diary in ink
take caution
before you adjust your space goggles
and dive back through time
where my history swirls with spirit dust
entangled in crystals dangling
silk-soaring out of the lava of others

THE ONES THAT MADE THEIR MARK

traveling moments that were ephemeral
you'll see that for a page or two
shiver gold and sing suspended
sky shifting through sunset
filmed forevermore.

UNDER THE LOVE OF ROOTS

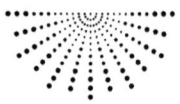

LIMITED EDITION

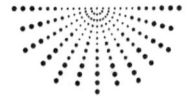

She was a girl whose
tuned-in heart was embossed with
that whistle-bellow steam of
the Belle of Louisville
and middle school class trips on boats
the footsteps of lovers kissing hands
tomorrow dreams glazed on sunset shoulders
apple-pie-eyed on the Big Four Bridge
the garlic salt and white pepper chatter
of fried chicken talking to the kitchen
those Louisville-favorite Hot Browns
hitting the spot for foodies
since a chef named Fred
first cooked up legend in the 1920s
and Southern hospitality basketed
in cream candy sayings
if you could just hold it
unbridled

in your sea salt hands
for safekeeping
you'd see it all
dripping with this world's waterfalls:
Oh those Kentucky winds.
They move close
and have their
creek-smoked
glassy julep ways
with you
with us
minted forever.
No matter how the dashing seas
turn
wanderer toes
blue;
No matter how his sleeveless eyes
turn
waffled feelings green
trickled to indigo ink.

You know,
that bluegrass kind of
Derby rose castle
velvet through two horse rib cages:
Just how a sparkling laugh
feels like corn whiskey
bold as
flirting in a bottle, magnificent
smack-dab during Prohibition,
starting gates loaded
cork ready to shoot

THE ONES THAT MADE THEIR MARK

the sound of *pow*
hooves to air and
swish brunette sass.

She liked her books
like she liked her
bourbon;
beautiful, neat,
sweet as a well-aged promise
so many stories
warm and nutty
apricot and hay rides
caramel earthy deep
as vanilla spice snapping
barrel words yet to be poured
on her tongue
page after page
note after note
toasted
tastes that linger
distilled
on an
oaken shelf.

Anything eager and gritty.
The jump of an entreaty.

Tuned-in to that luxe
kind of love
evergreen in a glass,
ageless in a hardback,
signed wet

lingering toasted true,
wheat-gold
or anywhere ocean
waiting for that
windy blue.

Beholden to
the *bite*.

I'LL TELL YOU A SECRET...

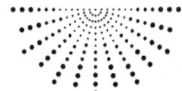

MY HEART KNOWS HOW TO GLOW IN THE DARK

I want to sip that North Star
clean through a straw.
Let the stardust
tingle; to the tip
of my tongue. Fizzling like soda
pop; smacking my lips- sighing
hydrogen to helium
through my teeth.

I sing in summerlike bubbles.
My anthems
catch on carbonated clouds.
Gummy daydreams turn saffron-rose-
in the open-mouthed
blue.

I guzzle that
wandering star

outside in,
until my heart-glow
finds a twin
steamed up
in the twinkle-looking glass,
sun-kissing the dark.

And here's the secret
to flying through midnight
to giving a starfish
aviation wings
water purring
under its breath below
moon doors unlocked
swinging wide
to a celestial city life-sized:
I swallow it
whole.

I PROMISE TOMORROW I'LL BE ZEN

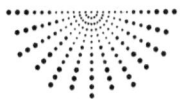

Sometimes I want to throw
my grating parmesan patience
like spaghetti carbonara
whisked eggs against the wall-
Just to watch the oregano jettison
in one fistful.

It's all salt and pepper to me.
Basta, basta.

Today I want a Michelangelo miracle-
A miracle ordered over easy;
The winged angelic
liberated
up a Sistine ceiling,
like yolk from the pearl.

Give me a six ounce can of
green karma, stewed in olive oil
diced like mind peppers
roasted angst I can chew,
sensitivity sizzling
a lemon-peeled delicacy-
Just let the butter foam.

Sour cream attitude,
stir it right in.
I'm over here riled up, elbows out.
Stainless steel
draining pasta water
billowing
absolutely boiling
trying to hammer out Renaissance
from sleeping rock.

Sometimes I feel like this skillet-
Sweating, tossed up in the air
Basilica to sky-painted wings
tangy and creamy.

Juicy
consciousness
bleeding tomato-
I palpitate parsley.
Don't mind me today
tender
raw
edges not quite gold

THE ONES THAT MADE THEIR MARK

not ready to cool:
Don't stick a fork in me,
noodles tied up
a busy dish undone.

THE FIRST FRIEND I MADE

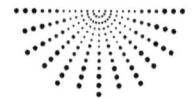

Pecan-knit pieces
thick as feel-good thieves
the gooey Derby pie fresh out
soothing and nutty
not just lucky things like
where a mother
hangs her fascinator in May
make up home
the anthem winds of green
summer rock n' roll combing through
a swaying backyard
a dandelion's freedom
feels like big-hearted clouds
watch over this personal jungle
an omnium gatherum
leafed clovers
dancers in the suburbs
grown for those days of young.

THE ONES THAT MADE THEIR MARK

Home finds its way like
the land of sisters
shared from different roofs
asphalt shingle neighbors
protecting scattered brick
learning the earth beneath
can make a backyard dance
an omnium gatherum
in leafed clovers
always underfoot
tender no matter the where
fountains paths
draw personal jungles
cloud angels watching over us
whispering new knowings
like Double Dutch ropes
promising flight to the sidewalks
we minted with chalk treasures
sisters like land to the red deer
seeing doe eyes in a creek
off the beaten track
growing into and beyond
those days of young.

That first friend
meeting and knowing
love sincere
the innocence of Barbie
moving dreamboats and Beanie Babies
hugging a small otter named Seaweed
her plush dog named Bones
placed at the top of the Christmas tree

how hickory wood floor
the here and there
carpet whistle-stop
suddenly turned to orbiting lava
remember how a pink leather couch
in a jump
became Pocahontas
singing out
under a weeping willow
to each color of the skating wind
for a beautiful time
we're unafraid-
such a piece
of serendipitous home;
a playful sanctuary
where friendship teaches
that some family
we choose.

Love unconditional
when there are no ties of ancestry
just scrunchies in our hair-
the first time
we see
what it's like to be
accepted entirely
to talk and jump
to roll in the personal jungle
to laugh in an omnium gatherum
in leafed clovers
some we wish on

THE ONES THAT MADE THEIR MARK

some we wish up
to the wind unafraid
happy as we are
asphalt shingle neighbors
protecting scattered brick
two young sister hearts
feeling separate and whole
we come to embrace
every piece
that makes up the home
of another.

What a gorgeous refuge
prettier than
a Barbie dreamboat
just home from the store
when we realize
at age five-
some family we get to choose.

The first friend
doesn't hammer
she shapes
like small hands in a
splashing pool
the first piece of a
heart that forms
outside of brick
outside of blood,
outside of traditions passed
from different

brick to blood and back-
an omnium gatherum
in leafed clovers
jungle exploration
growing free
that whooshing infinite
childhood magic
it erases hickory limitations
and gives instead
a companion
to brave the jump
into any wind's wild unafraid.

I'd remember anywhere
the smiling face
underneath happy blonde hair,
the love I have
for my first friend
she shared first moments
of dreamboat imagination
backyard-giggling,
discovering a jungle world close
through lash-bouncing firefly eyes
those chicken baccata days
where what we didn't finish
shimmied in a sink burble down
where we hid M&Ms behind plants
that love, that home
that kindergarten young
seed moments grew sanctuary
staying underfoot
like the depths of laughter

THE ONES THAT MADE THEIR MARK

could take root for miles
protecting scattered brick
fountain of paths
taking that omnium gatherum
in dreams-made-real clovers
land of sisters
we held in hands that splashed
innocence in whirlpools
it stayed with us.

I'm 32 now
and though I no longer hide
M&Ms that dropped
behind potted plants
I sing out evergreen memory
like homecomings
brick sanctuaries shaped in sister winds
noticing how decades later
I love the asymmetrical
in this omnium gatherum
where dancers in cities nod to suburbs
I can hang my hats in colors unafraid
a suitcase of childhood I carry
dreams unzipped
like Double Dutch ropes
promising flight to sidewalks
patterned in chalk hymns
giving grace to the earth.

The days of young remain
I hold onto them all this time
protecting lands that made us

my scattered paths
her rich laughter
firsts and follies:
It's sacred knowing
some family
we've chosen.

EVEN IN SECOND GRADE

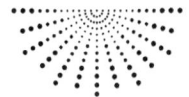

Mrs. Walker furrowed her
pearl-gray brow
arched
like a Robin Hood arrow
point-blank
through King John's nobility
a moment of decorum usurped:
"Your pilgrims are historically inaccurate."
I gave them red lips.
In her eyes,
I might as well have just nocked the arrow
a seven-year-old archeress that frustrated her
to no creative end
every day that school year.

She wanted each of us
to box our pilgrims
into black and white symmetry-

No room for salt kissing pepper
my jaunty Thanksgiving dimension
landing a paso doble
mid-scene
must have shimmered obnoxious,
as Mrs. Walker certainly scrambled
a whole Ohio River
and then some short on patience
for my incompatible
ruby and aquamarine
enthusiasm bedazzling the Mayflower
Plymouth to Plymouth in 1620.

Her Oregon Trail-sized problem was:
There I tickled crayons past
the rectangular page,
arbitrary horizontal lines in place
for me to jump around
pine cone suggestions
I frankly didn't take
not even as young'un gospel-
How could I?
I was imagining my pilgrims
touching the vitality of berries
juice balm to their adventurer mouths
already seeing a good way off
from elementary barriers
conjuring clear of all grayscale
drawing the New World in rainbow.

POLISHED

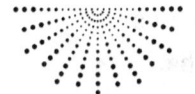

Before I lived in Israel,
I used to adore the lightbulb thrill
of straightening my Jewish hair
curls that otherwise
would stick out like such a shock
when the *thinner* and *straighter*,
the magazines told us, the better
we can potion ourselves into beautiful:
so I painted a flamingo a sleek silver
hid any startling pink in sight
and like a lampshade
for a brief moment
I turned myself out
to turn the acceptance of the crowd on
with vertical hurrahs.

'Why don't you wear your hair like that
all the time? You look amazing!

You're Anne Hathaway'
and I'd respond,
'I'm my mom's Anne Hathaway'
because my mother adores me
just as I am
natural curls a gift of legacy and spirit
she gave to me the day I was born
and when I had straight bangs
as a child, she'd curl my hair
behind my ears
seeing the wild that already was brewing
on the top of my tiny head
hair that seemed to transform
into zigs and zags
bursting through the years
as if my biggest thoughts
stretched from my mind
right into free-for-all
excitement down my spine.

I'd iron the flamingo right out of me
because as a teen
the worst thing you can do
is not fit in
and as an adult
you carry those kinds of oversights
even when you finally learn to unpack
it's just a suitcase of worsts turned
pieces we come to leave open
in the corner of who we become
beautiful whether the magazines
give us grace

THE ONES THAT MADE THEIR MARK

or banish us as the loud, pink flamingos
our untamed joys really are.

It wasn't until I walked off the plane
in a land of camels, hi-tech rises, and desert euphoria
where curls bounced
like humps on camels
carrying water
to soothe suitcases full of forgotten thirst
flamingo pinks everywhere
bright as UV rays
a free-for-all
boys looked at me like I was
and not just all I wasn't but could be
if I just ironed out my worsts and zags
and I felt new excitement
like dazzling water circling down my spine.

I took my suitcases home with me
when I flew
back from one home to another
and didn't just leave them in the corner
I wore what was inside
in the heart of Kentucky
feeling every inch
of un-straightened legacy
the spirit I was meant to love
because it's a gift from my mother
who traveled from Ecuador here
suddenly it's all mine
in whole new zigs and zags
and it's shockingly glorious

when I just let the light stay on
and don't hide my curled flamingo leg
behind a crowd of silvers
that are probably so bright
when they're not trying to gray themselves
into upstanding and controlled lines.

It's been some time now
since I felt the compulsion
to direct my wild into movie star straw
letting the water dance across
the desert spots
hot pink and outright electric thrills
until Diana was ready
to walk down a cinematic aisle
and she kindly gestured in a text
with the assumption
that I was
already thinking of straightening my hair,
right?

It hit me like a ton of old flamingos
gone hiding
pointing at suitcases
I thought I'd unlocked
because for the first special event
in many lightbulbs blinked out
I really hadn't.

It could be anything,
she assured me
just be polished

THE ONES THAT MADE THEIR MARK

just don't be bohemian
and I couldn't help thinking
it felt like don't be curly
don't be wavy
don't be a flamingo
like you used to be
but I still was
and am
and was born to be
so what a collision
suitcases and souvenirs
to find myself staring at magazines
moving pictures in my mind
wondering what about my wild
triggered this anxiety
for such a spectacular moment in her life
someone I love with worlds and hearts
flamingo leg days like a ripple.

Am I polished?
Can I pretend to be polished
for a day
knowing this would bring water
to what makes my friend evermore
feel afraid
can I support her fairytale joys
even if I iron out the camel humps
the flamingo wiggles
the light that sticks just a little too out?

The truth is
I wonder if it would erase my discoveries

to travel back to days of vertical
pretend to be polished
for a day
but I also see
that even someone as beautiful
as Diana
with golden locks straight
and a heart that turns happiness on
might be carrying suitcases
that she hasn't unzipped
and I think that no matter
if I zig or zag
or play Anne Hathaway in *Polished*
I know that with me
she doesn't have to hide
her rough edges
her fears and non-cinematic real
in a corner
and whatever I do
I'll be a flamingo in front of a crowd
light beautiful and on
watching the tears
curl in her brilliant eyes.

AIRPORTS AND TABASCO DREAMS

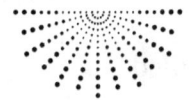

Rose boots wink
clap-tapping
through
the hot buzz
goodbyes that chatter
even the sound of hugs echo
well-built forever moments in
the Trevi fountain of navy
passed-around passports today,
talk tomorrow, talk as soon as we land
the cranium of airport halls, like
mozzarella drumming atop pasta.
Gooey
and delicious
quicksilver percussion.

How it feels when you're about to fly.

The hair on the nape of your neck
rises
celery stalks shooting invisible
but water beads real on excited skin,
seat belts
snap-click in salty seconds.
This plane rumbles like a
big meatball
appetite loud as wishes pulled
pooled
from childhood
when I first flew at 9 months-old
before I had spaghetti words
for the heartbeat of travel feelings,
hot marinara chasing
into the sky.

Precious luggage in the belly
something inherited
from hungry women before me
percussive heartbeats
red Ecuadorian scarves knit in mountains
Chimborazo and Galapagos footsteps
that once sounded out hope
by hopping on a flight
my grandmother with sapphire eyes
Eastern-European feisty from Slovakia
my grandfather I never met from Hungary
who once hid his luggage
precious diamond in his tooth
to gift generations the revelation of living
like the Nazi who set him free

THE ONES THAT MADE THEIR MARK

because my Opi Pablo saved a life
precious to that Nazi
and because of all that
because of footsteps
and the hope it takes to travel
the pangs of hunger and wanting
something that could be inherited
my mother from Quito who carried
my Opi Pablo's luggage
soft, respectable leather
to study English in a land of dreams
as far as Opi Pablo saw it
as far as I'm told
my mother who fell in love
with my father in Louisville
like the photo shows in the basement collage
noodled in warmth of the same red scarf
precious love from different lands
different hungers, different wanting
shared all because my mother took a plane
all because my grandparents took a plane
all because my Opi Pablo saved a life
and saved our lives
and me
raised with the mistiness of
Now Boarding
the jump and jolt of adventure.

I can feel the all-out pause
the softness of
bread-dough-waiting
a stream of seconds

shaken out
like olive oil
tongue-tied
taking a
slow
voyage breath
as if it chooses to hit the pan
just-so
meditating on past lives
when its olives were handpicked
bitter-loves paste-spun
at high-velocity
tight *exhilarating* suspension
time-honored
nutrients we come to know
tasted between teeth
meeting and greeting
what's bitter turns divine
so much found
in between sundial ticks and tocks
salty snap-clicks and *buckle-up*
what a zingy parenthesis release
airplane thoughts
whooshing
where mozzarella drummed
up to this now
on the winds of moving sidewalks
the flush of the rush
that fast simmer of travel time
szzzzzh
now brought to a purling standstill
the rumba of the Pentagons

THE ONES THAT MADE THEIR MARK

shuffled about intel flitting in
and out of purses
over rigatoni arms
through thyme security
shoved pasta-tight in
nearby overhead bins
in the twinkle of Tabasco,
on the far side of
the cranium of airport halls
the before anything else
so deep below
a transcendent sense of
chapters lived
sponged up
in flush and drumsteps gone by
the speed of travel sound
and time
curving smoky
beneath the chill of metal
wavy rectangular seatbelts
reverberating
all that precious packed
in the belly of the plane
how it all stretches like
cheese hours.

If I dared, could I
scoop up sweet ricotta clouds
gooey like love and wanting
like histories and leather-life
swung precious in bare hands?
Just maybe.

Anything in this wild blue heaven
feels dolce vita-
I'm savoring
every meringue glance
every salty second
that's been passed down
scarves knit
neck to neck
with water beads- tall above
these Leonardo da Vinci wings.

I can almost taste the universe
courses scarfed down before
the rumble of what's to come,
red pepper flakes
twirled into garlic secrets.
Time zones
wind back like athletes
survivors and adventurers; effortless,
powerful. We lean forward
like a tower into the desert.
Faraway lands steal
close.

The plane strolls down the
windborne escalator
where dusk and memories prism
into
daylight
and how it seems to fly
like sugar and dynamite
acrobats from a polished spoon.

THE ONES THAT MADE THEIR MARK

I want
to let air
and *new*
drizzle
down my lungs, infinite. Satisfy
my hungry
gypsy soul
pack it in my luggage
and take it precious with me.

We cut through states and realms
smooth as tiramisu.
Soda cups don't rattle. But
the energy, the now of it all
zips in
percussive heart
in lusty
pops
of
altitude.

The sun dips along,
a summery, dawn-ready shine.
Gin-soaked
and ripe for the picking
for the carrying
in teeth
in inherited suitcases
bursting precious.

When this plane tumbles
down, it's pepper

making its move to the main
dish. And there,
just maybe,
you can spot me,
daughter of lovers across lands,
granddaughter of
those who lived, who hungered
to eat up this prism world
every last precious bite
who turned something bitter
dynamite gooey divine,
romantic and ravenous,
eyes that grew up searching past
the oval window: survivor-wild with
Tabasco dreams.

MY FAKE TAXI NAME IS RIVA

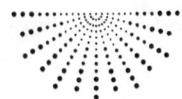

The first time I ordered
a taxi in Israel
it wasn't a ruse:
There really was a Riva
in my Destiny Yisrael program
and she really did need a taxi.
Why she didn't want to order
from her Irish cell phone
I never understood
but maybe that was part
of her mystery.
I saw a girl who had overstayed
her welcome at an apartment
I shared with seven others
who brought phones
from Hamburg
(he liked to remind me
he was actually born in Zurich)

from Palo Alto
ones who hated air conditioning
and others who craved it so much
they wanted mechanical air blasts
running into them like pomegranate wine
and undoubtedly those would be
the exact ones mismatched together
leaving the American from Connecticut
to sit in another room
square on the claustrophobic floor
just to feel the chill whisper
through the rickety Tel Aviv vents.
And then there was Riva.

Riva had stayed the night
because one of the million Alexes
Australian Boy Alex
he thought he'd get Irish lucky
with this one
because all he saw was a human thrill
when I saw a girl needing to need
so much so
she wanted to feel someone else
could order a cab for her
(or so I tell myself)
and because my heart broke
to see another mismatch unraveling
like air conditioning wars between
roommate Montagues and Capulets
and my heart broke
because I could tell
she couldn't see Australian Boy Alex's

THE ONES THAT MADE THEIR MARK

eyes static open with annoyance
the aggravation of feeling unlucky
the next morning
of being woefully reminded of it
before coffee could even speak out loud
Riva chattering at the crammed table
while others who've needed to be needed
forgot all those times
and silently condemned her
at the start of it all
I handed over a cell phone
from Kentucky
because sometimes typing in
another's name
feels like a digital gift
connecting needs
sharing the chill so it feels less cold
when another doesn't notice
skin rises like water hills on a camel's back.

I remembered not understanding
why my roommate could hate Riva
quite as much as she did
when she clearly had her own
need to feel needed
as I witnessed a Freudian relationship
unfold like the boxers out of the laundry
Haley would fold for the boys
like the Shabbat salads she'd make
jack-in-the-box heart shouting
pop goes the weasel
as she'd say *hashtag we needed this*

like the beds she'd share cuddling
with Australian Boy Sam and Joshua
after they'd all have dates
wanting to almost be their mother
and their quasi-lover
air conditioning blasting, of course.

Yet, Lord forbid
if Girl Alex D
has a dad who loves her
visiting
curious to learn where his daughter
will spend her next chapter of time
because now Alex D
gets branded the unfortunate nickname
of Alex Dad
as if that's the worst thing in the world
to have a caring dad present-
and it dawns on me
that maybe it is for someone like Haley
whose family relationships are strained
shut into the cupboard
away from Mesa dinners
only when she's not hating me
enough to tell me
for me to see self-hatred stirs
like the salad she mixes
like the 'I love her to *death*, **but!**'
she throws out
as soon as Alex Robin
has the nerve to ask to go skydiving
with Haley and Lacey

THE ONES THAT MADE THEIR MARK

the New Hampshire *nerve*
something that stays a secret
from Alex Robin
who everyone shortens to just Robin
which feels infinitely cooler
than Alex Dad,
which is a shame,
because I remember Alex Dad
wore a fabulous pop of eyeliner
and there were other things to notice
about her.

I kept Riva's name in my back pocket
even after her Israel journey
came to a traumatic end
in the Bat Yam house
she shared with the Bolivians
who had their own conflict
with the Chileans
and I seemed to jive with them all
que tals happily in Spanish
except the Americans
like the time I fled a city away
to escape my roommate's
bottleneck rage at my general existence
when she wanted the room
at all hours
because her younger Israeli crush
Hezi couldn't get it up
until after beer pong with his bros
only Haley for after
Haley when it was 5am

always Haley for the end
and Haley trying to gain control
any way she could
which was problematic
for a roommate like me
who'd eat many a pizza at 5am
wandering the streets
slice of Tony Vespa getting my hands
good and midnight-greasy
joking I escaped to the
'Bat Yam Witness Protection Program'
accepting dates that felt
more like being kidnapped
like the physicist in Haifa
whose sister looked at me
with sand-blown skepticism
salty in her eyes
searching me to find out
why was I there
and I couldn't help wanting to answer
I felt the same existential dread
and it sure felt like Haley did too.

It wasn't until the end
that Riva's experience collided
like a truck of paint
crashed right into Habima Square
and it was hard to make out
cold paint splatter from growing flowers
the Bolivians all screaming
about the cat! the cat!!!
and a text message lights up

THE ONES THAT MADE THEIR MARK

my cell phone from Kentucky
in Tel Aviv
a phone with Riva's name
written out in the taxi app
about a calamity occurring in Bat Yam
because a girl from Dublin
is trying to drown a cat in
a scalding sink full of apartment water-
And I can't help feeling appalled.

Riva had learned
that when a cat like this one
is blind and hurting
you help that street-wounded animal
by killing off its pain
just put the kitty out of its awful misery.
And to this day
it breaks my heart
not even just that a girl like Riva
could think that's the best way
to confront suffering
but it made me think
about how much of her pain
her need
she wished she could drown
throw it all down the sink, hot
gone.

So when the taxi drivers
later would ask me
what my name was
I'd say Riva with *emphasis*

like a Kentucky-Israeli
and I'd weave a glittering tale
a story of rehabilitation
well, that only I would know
each taxi ride a different tale of legend
because I never want to become
so ruthless
that I forget to look pain in the eye
even if it's sore and blind
I never want to brand someone
by whose parent has loved them up
and whose parent has taught them
only to drown.

BUY THE DRESS COVERED IN ROSE PETALS

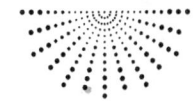

Family legend has it
my Opi Pablo sketched a ring
a doctor who had to repeat
his boards over again
in Ecuador
after making it out
of World War II Hungary
free from Nazis
doctor's pen to
loose-leaf paper
before he could afford it:
And he told my Neny,
'One day this will be yours.'
And so it was,
that one day,
the loving sketch
of that paper ring
fluttered off the page

a juicy jewel
saved like an architect
a curator of time's beauty sleep
onto my Neny's
sun-speckled finger.

I know because she told me-
and when I was very young,
even though I never knew
my mother's father,
my Opi Pablo,
who my brother Paul
was named after
I knew my Neny,
and I knew what it meant
to be
dream-it-on-paper
pride-nurtured
like roses grown
in Ecuadorian soil
that resplendent equator sun
month-of-Sundays-waiting
make-it-all-real
kind of generous.
Neny always told me
that's the best kind of man-
And so I believed her
with all my green heart.

I grew up spending
summers
generous with adventure

THE ONES THAT MADE THEIR MARK

trying out leather coats
made by hand in Otavalo
hearing Quechua in the markets
and offers to buy 'sandía, sandía!'
fresh watermelon for a deal
right outside the windows
of the wooden house
where my mother grew up
a dream doctors didn't believe
could come true for my Neny
family full of miracles
inside all that magnificent wood
Ecuadorian roses blazing red
and sparkling pink by the pool
guanabana and chocolate
ice cream cones
melting in our hands
my grandmother who
would share
her favorite accessories with me
who only ever looked beautiful
eyes like jewels designed on paper
and would teach me to be the one
who orders dessert first
when out for lunch with friends.

I learned to be warm
as the equator sun
like a cone for
the Cotopaxi
a volcano
permanently covered

in snow,
where even when
the peak is cold forever
the lava erupted in 1877
among other vivacious times
lava's dream manifested
melting snow and ice
to a mudflow racing
sometimes I imagine
as if it must have cheered
in Spanish,
'Soy libre!'
because even fire can feel free
ice can feel its generosity
and sometimes
a dream-made-real
has some sudden mudflows
to spring it off paper
like a moving volcano
cheers in Spanish
all those years after
it spent hibernating,
conjuring in the waiting.

The house was a dream
which seemed to be how
Opi Pablo
must have quietly spoken
his love aloud
to my Neny
and I wonder if her beauty
made him want to meet

THE ONES THAT MADE THEIR MARK

the sapphire dazzle
that bounced
with flecks of coral
in her eyes
and some shards of ice hidden
as her own remnants
carried silently from the war
not shown to us
only dreams manifested
through the
volcano-cheering fire
of jewel-toned liberty
every move she made
in a house
once just a
black-and-white sketch
on doctor's paper
echoing with the
rich wood of new beginnings
fought for
love abundant
miracles generous
even after so much ice
how I only saw the melting of it
when I'd fly miles and miles
to hold her sun-speckled hand.

We used to stream over memories
in photos that kept life alive
generous with smiles
and my Neny showed me
one of my absolute favorites

at the doctor's ball with Opi Pablo
where she looked like
Miss Universe
in a dress covered with roses.
Her taste in fashion was impeccable
Neny let her colors run bright as
equator-kissed flowers
free as lava melting ice peaks
and her coral-flecked
sapphires beamed eternal
in that moment
with pride to feel so beautiful
even for a dress she wore
just that one night.

My mother, a second miracle child
was raised with Opi Pablo's
hard-won dreams-off-paper
protective practicality
and questioned if it was worth it
one night
mud flows preceding
a dance in roses
bright even in black-and-white
and Neny cheered in Spanish
'Por su puesto!'
and glinted those jewel-joy eyes
at my green heart
learning life through
sleeping volcanoes and
happiness melting ice cream cones
sticky on my pale fingers

that wanted to be sun-speckled
like my Neny's
but my mom saw me as
a miracle's miracle's miracle
and she'd slather my pearl skin
in the highest SPF sun tan lotion
worried how the altitude
might catch my lungs
not used to the volcano peaks
and Neny told me:
'Ju-Ju, promise me
you'll buy the dress one day
covered in rose petals
and you'll celebrate
how beautiful it is
to be a dancing flower
even for a night.'

I made that promise-
I believed everything
my Neny taught me
because she made her lessons
look as beautiful
as roses that
came of new reckoning
along the equator
and that was after
forever ice
the kind that never fully melts
but she lived with lava racing
and Opi Pablo sharing his miracles
his love and liberty with her

with wood-sturdy generosity
from paper to a house
that would raise
the next generation
and meet his spirit
through dreams-made-real
and that's why
I bought the yellow-strappy heels
just to walk through the Colosseum
the beautiful history in cobblestones
when I'd walk
ice cream cone melting in my hand
under a faraway sun
shining down
on a Kentucky miracle in Rome.

DEAR WONDER LOVE OF MY LIFE

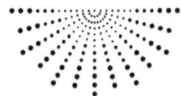

(WHEREVER YOU ARE)

Sometimes I wonder love
strolling through the halls
of my kintsugi heart
that spreads gold gusto wings
uplifted in the broken ache spaces:
What cheese do you like today
that yesterday you hadn't
run your strawberry rhubarb jelly
tongue up against to try
mouth unraveling
the cheesemaker's delicately
sought after balance?

When I was 10,
I skinned my knee
right on the speckled cobblestones
playing on the twins' sidewalk
who lived across the street

and I saw the reddest rivers
leaking
forming tributaries
black and blue grand canyons
my right knee so pale next to
all that flesh gashed
in ribbons as if a scissor curled them
and I saw my father so scared
to see me hurting
that he vowed never to teach me
to ride a bicycle-
Really, all he ever wanted
in our loving world
spinning or still
was the earthly power
the pizza recipe for fathers and daughters
the wherewithal to protect me,
his "girlie."

The remnants of rivers
once brick-red three
now one leftover cut
marking childhood days
invisible to almost anyone else
but maybe you
still kisses the center
of my left knee.
What history scrolls
like horseshoes hiding
on your kneecaps
that one day I'll kiss
with softest rootless lips

THE ONES THAT MADE THEIR MARK

searching to water every scar
like nostalgia rolling deep
juicy asparagus
waiting to pop out
harvest moon
sage scattered
sprouty treasures
palms grasping the countryside?

In middle school,
smack dab in the middle
of my purple-green braces
those buried awkward years
alive as any old scar on my legs,
a bully almost spat the words:
"*Your hair looks like your head exploded,*"
and it felt like a hailstorm of awful
churning disappointment in my stomach
down at the mango oblong pit of it
where I first learned how cruel boys
carrying secret acid pain
like math books making backpacks heavy
can be to a bright-hot blue-star daydreamer
like me.

Have you ever been so surprised,
your bright-hots, your illusions,
your braces and your old new scars
have engulfed you
like a mean twister eats a power line?
I didn't buy a yearbook that year.

One day I'll tell you how many times
I've cut my hair.
For years, I would grow it Disney-princess-long
so I could cut it off for Locks of Love
hoping cancer patients could
feel the weight of it
like the safety of disappearing inside
a pages-long fairytale.
The first time I cut it all off for me
was after my first heartbreak-
I lopped it into a bob
wanting to look in the mirror
and find myself unrecognizable
from the girl who carried her first love's
pain for far too long.

As a child, my hair barely curled,
a smile looped just under my ears,
bangs my mother cut
so she could see the joy dance
toasted chocolate in sensitive eyes.
I only grew it out
because my Bubby told me then
I could wear a scrunchie
and I thought maybe then she would love me
because it felt like she was sometimes
the only grandparent that didn't
and wonder love,
that hurt worse than the knee;
A hurt I swallowed because I love my father
so much I'd drink back bloody tributaries
if I could protect him.

THE ONES THAT MADE THEIR MARK

Wonder love,
I want you to know
that my Bubby soul-open loved my father
with the Willie Nelson-melodies best of her
love she'd saved like lost riches
during the Great Depression
where her mother Selma
wished on rabbits' feet.
She gave my brother,
all the boys, really
the best of her
in weekly Shabbat dinner conversations
and even though I loved her
only to be the one to find
the unblunted fragments of her
like a shocking Picasso painting
most don't see under the socks in the drawer
I didn't let that make up the worst of me;
And maybe that's because
my father has loved me
with the steady best of him
and I love that that pours
from her well of love
though some waters
felt like lost riches to me
no matter how many times
I tried to access with a pump
with pipes-
and I know that makes up
some of the best of me
anyway.

When I was four,
the pre-school teacher realized
if she sat me next to
the troubled kid in class,
those sour, asymmetrical moments
stirred sweet as homemade lemonade.
I can imagine it
as if his tartish eyes let out bubbles
when we'd talk-
I wonder if that's all that was missing,
someone who would notice
if he was blinking back brine
or letting the marrow of him
feel tenantless
just for a nurtured time and space
among paint-chips
and tiny wooden chairs.
They called it "Beauty and the Beast;"
and I learned by four
that my job was to soak up
all the lemon in sight,
blend it in my pitcher,
make it drinkable for everyone.

At the age of 30,
I started to learn that
I don't have to sweeten up
every beastly moment I meet.
But I know we can take
all the sour that we've faced
and it's nonetheless a beautiful thing
to know how to taste the nuance

THE ONES THAT MADE THEIR MARK

to let it linger behind cold teeth
and drink in the asymmetry
of worlds together and apart
like this is all our sparkling lemonade.
I know there's a difference now
between tartish have to and
refreshing want to-
And together, we can
let out the bubbles
whenever we talk.

Sometimes I wonder love,
will we meet in this paella life
or the next morsel of universe-side
basketful of paprika lessons learned?
Do you ever miss your first love's family?
I sure do- I think of his mother
soft, honest smile
daylight in the kitchen
turning black bananas into
banana bread passed hand to open hand
that could melt beaten egg conflicts
clinging in the air between cupboards
into buttered brown sugar.
I think of his Nana who taught us
Italian spaghetti and meatballs
could grin with secret raisins
and it all made intriguing sense
for a chewy mouthful
well-seasoned history passed forward
hands to mouths
my ex's temper forgotten

in the background of these memories.

And how for my brother
it's all a heartfelt sibling punchline
seven years later at the dinner table
over falafel and cucumbers.
How my brother married his first love
so there are years and slices I think
he'll never understand of me
even though there are years
only he will gather our family's ingredients
like no one else can
and his wife with turquoise aurora
warm in her eyes
serves pumpkin bread
careful when she cuts a piece straight
love that doesn't crumble
but feels like kitchen daylight
in my nephews' laughing bellies.

When you were a kid on the playground,
did you watch ants scatter
and hope they made it home
summer heat dancing
like childhood spotlights on pavement
underground tunnels safe
back to their families
carrying cracker crumbs?
My father will tell me
the mosquitoes bite
"Because you're so sweet,"
and when the world bites

THE ONES THAT MADE THEIR MARK

my mother tells me,
"I'm sorry I gave you my heart."
And I answer back
Ecuador mountains heart
passed between open hands:
"I'm not."

Do you think about
what can make us feel
like we're paralyzed
salmon to a fisherman's hook
snap-caught on the outside looking in
how just from one stitch of waves
one group of people to the next
that stark gap between
closed-off clique
everyone but you knowing
each other's soda orders
where it feels like your personality
somehow gets bleached into oblivion
the discomfort of feeling jagged
a chink in an othered fence-
How much better it fills
the meeting of open eyes
open souls wafting
hands that have somehow passed
like-minded hearts forward
how when you're apart of
the lace-work of connection
even when the circle is new
raw truths can caramelize
the flavor of authentic conversation

crunchy as candy apples in the fall?
Suddenly
we're walking home in freckled skin
a gallery of happy again
the "you're welcome here"
seeing from the inside
deep thought blooms unafraid within
vulnerability sewn as an electric-blanket
keeping us warm laughing bellies-up
the kaleidoscope joy of looking out
sanctuary in togetherness
playing "tag-you're-it"
with all the zig-zag colors
a grateful place for the all of it
feelings of time to spare
watching planes braiding the clouds above.
The first time I felt that
I remember wanting to give a hug
at a family party
and an adult sternly telling me
frown carefully tight:
"We don't hug; we shake hands."
I still feel like I want to hug
every human I meet
until they prove to me
they're a hand-shaker;
And I learn to open difference
as there's astronomical room
for tight bear hugs
that could take on
an entire looming forest
and those who carry shards of pain

THE ONES THAT MADE THEIR MARK

frozen like a bag of peas
I may never understand
and would rather keep
electric vulnerability
at a safer distance.

Wonder love, do you think
we've been connected
at the seams of breaths and wishes
all these years before
like a bee hive of Quito lights
whispering a flutter of shimmer
throwing a current of glow
angels of the city holding up the dark
the first starlit landmark view
I couldn't wait to see
each passing June
outside the airplane window
just before landing
the way lightning
dazzle-hugs the ground?
I spent some of my favorite nights
staying up
as if powered by moonwake
lost in books and flashlights
fingers caressing black ink
springing off pages, pages
flipping
musing
wading through stories
past writers' dreams
forwards and backwards

hands to mind
wide-open.
But I've learned some things
you can't learn in beautiful hardbacks
some things you can only learn
through the touch of skin reading skin
and mouths devouring dawn
on the other side of the world
and back again
through river homecomings
sweeping upwards
like corn stalks rising
just-rained green at the farmhouse
near the home my parents raised me.

When we find each other
somewhere somehow
vulnerability wholly electric
will we light each other up
inside out
like Quito from an airplane
bending the throttle
landing awake at nightfall?
Are we making our way through
pages ever-turning pages
stories cooking saucy dreams
frozen handshakes and hello-again hugs
Galapagos tortoise backwards
lighting-kissing-the-ground forward
looking out the fogged-up window
where breaths and wishes feel seen
until we can read one another's skin

THE ONES THAT MADE THEIR MARK

city angels holding up our hearts?

I keep thinking it's you
with a just-rained bright grin
and I'm over here
Kentucky bluegrass finding a way
dreaming up
through
precious cracks in pavement
making asphalt my ladder
master of green-rising:
All I need is an opening.
But time and time again,
it isn't you-
Not yet.
He's a misty almost
a mythical never-was
hypnotic as slipping sand
and I'm either basking
in the ghost aftershock
of a terrible won't be
or left putting the bolt to my mouth
of all his brilliant hurt-me-deep.

Wonder love, where are you tonight?
Are you looking at your shadow
how it casts a living image
a blurred confidante
tied to your gathering darkness
a sock hop under the streetlights?
Are you cradling bourbon's
bass-string quiver

amber over ice cubes
getting its bearings
clear as a twist whiskey glass
crystal-cut as a first time?

I was 20 the first time I got drunk
so bashful about that New Year's kiss
I thought I could forge
an invisible liquid shield
between malted Blue Moon
Belgian White beers
our lips impermeable to the crowd.

Even then I knew
tiger's eye opening passion
first-love heart
never quite woken up like this before
yearning spangled in goosebumps
like bourbon ice down my early 20s arms:
Some moments you share like soda pop orders
but some you keep close to your
heart to hands
invisible under a greenhouse
two eyes drunk on the blue moons in his.

Some geyser moments
get to be sipped special
don't you think?
like purple sun empires
and one day
I'll carry my Ecuador mountains heart
all that patchwork green and gold

THE ONES THAT MADE THEIR MARK

to your open hands
like years-aged bourbon
in passed-forward crystal.

Maybe then we'll both share
soda pop orders
spangled in urgent goosebumps
oh at last
at last
at last
and I'll say, *"there you are"*
our passion love
generous as corn stalks rising
wonder, yours and mine
of your before and my after
impermeable to a crowd
vulnerability electric as
airplanes landing
even in the ache spaces
where open tiger eyes turn them golden
that kind of Happy-New-Year-invincible
unforgettable
grass after years of rain
making the tallest greenhouse home
courageous right through the deepest cracks
and we'll read each other's stories
we won't need flashlights anymore
we'll feel each other's dreams on
bass-string quiver skin
just like a first time
the first time we find each other
frozen handshakes melting

like purple sun empires in our mouths
shadows and streetlights and starlight
breaths and wishes colliding
wings over blue moons
the way we'll hold lightning gentle
awake
as we dazzle-hug the ground.

MAY YOUR LOVE GROW FLYING

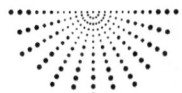

(FOR LEAH AND BRETT)

May your love grow wings
flying in a great splash
of feathery hope
that magical fluff
that lifts earth hearts tall as dreams
and keeps soul bonds warm in winter.

May your love compass in bark
soaring circles within
the kind that tell tree stories
of ancient and new
that beautiful cocoon
that shields lovers through the ages
and plants wild roots in summer fields.

May your love dive through seas of seven
swimming beside mermaid songs
the ones that hum turquoise and magenta

that bubbly *whoosh*
that guides humans to laugh below tides
nightingales to whistle atop sunsets
and shows legends how to wiggle toes
wading fantasy through reality
tending autumn's crops marked in gold.

May your love grow flying
until even Everest looks up
that enchanted knowing
winking in snow-capped awe.

A NARRATOR'S FAIR WARNING

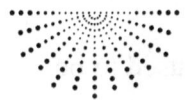

They say *be careful what you wish for*
and yet I grew up belly full of fish wishes
rippling planets about
a bubble bath of be-careful's
fins that sent me snorkeling tall
I can tell
they didn't get that right.

No, my favorite reader
be careful instead not what you wish
but what you *read*
because even the most honest truth-sayer
might be painting with fishtail reflections
where on the ripple backwards
some of the illumination ends up taking
a wish-net full of eclipse-
where her moment of sooth-storying
might travel from here to Neptune

and land tomorrow
in a cosmonaut float
belly full of bubbles and let-us-be's.

It's not that my hips weren't standing
when I told you:
It's that today when I recount it all
my spirit backpacks
right where my wish feet used to be.

Be careful what you read-
My truth might be another's departure;
Alaska and the Middle East
yarn in suns apart.

INSURRECTION

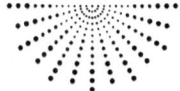

It's a domino
they don't watch snapshots
how one makes them fall

THE BROKEN PLATES

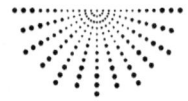

'She shouldn't have placed
the plates there,'
the family whispered
in that decibel tone
that spiteful gossip
fuels
like a glockenspiel
over the sound of
my mother's plates
as they cracked
against
our square pink
kitchen tiles
in a roll
a fold
a countless coming apart.

I can see my mother's

THE ONES THAT MADE THEIR MARK

movie star mole on her cheek
the cinema of entertaining
like broken ceramics
staying in cracked place.

I'm back to eight years old
hearing my family tell
Mrs. Navi
'It's her fault you broke
her plates.'
I see the rush
in a Disney lion stampede
plates collapsing
like the strike of hyenas
in an outrageous blur.

I think of my father at a wedding
where someone crashes wine
into his starched white collar
his suit in between dancing
at the table of guests
and family says to the
wine-spiller
not to fix it
to do nothing
as the wine looks
like my father is bleeding
and how for my father
he'd give the starched shirt
off his back
just if he could help
justice painting him

like a mural of red wine.

I think of all the times
plates are broken
and the wine gets
bloody on a suit
and how families
how worlds
seem spliced
with those who do the cracking
the staining
and those who clean up
what's messy and shattered
even if the place
where they're standing
and sitting
has nothing to do
with the breaking
the contaminating
at all.

SKETCHING TALES

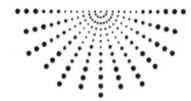

'You know, your father's not a prince,'
you once told me.
When I was little, you spun a tale
a tall, wild thing
that it was a jaws-shut family secret
my mother and father running away
like an Ecuadorian telenovela
the Spanish daughter
of a European doctor
into the arms of an American lawyer
eloping without anyone the wiser
and the way you hand-sketched
legend had it
my Neny was so beside herself
with great displeasure
that my parents had to be wed twice.

This is what outings together

sometimes (often) were like
although I doubt you'd remember.
As I grew older, my eyes widened less
and honestly when I heard
that my father was not your idea
of a crowned prince
it didn't really surprise me
because in your telenovela
my mother and father
they could never be the heroes
and it makes sense now
because when you've spent
your whole life
not feeling like the legend you know
you are
sometimes it must feel nice
to fabricate some tales
some tall, wild things
where for once you get to spin truths
to fit feelings that maybe have been
shoved aside
without anyone the wiser.

Here I come along
the daughter of a woman you wish
was the runaway
the daughter of a man
you won't curtsy to
even though truth is
he'd never ask that
because my father himself would say
he's no prince

THE ONES THAT MADE THEIR MARK

even though in my legend he's an Atticus
and I see a woman
who's not so different than a young child
unable to carry a tapestry of emotions
acting out but then when you leave
she's sad to see you go
and I think of our inner children
that we too often are told
to push into adulthood
how growing up you're praised
if you're behaving like a 'big girl'
and how many tiaras get lost
when we lock our youth away
only to rattle in our hearts
in languages some forget how to speak.

I know that complicated protagonist
she's in there
even still
after many snide passing remarks
about princes
and lies about telenovelas that
didn't quite happen the way you wish
in reality
I sometimes see the
child that must have been
who got to wear the golden tiara
and paint oak with a dazzle of feisty spice
I hear her when you make us all laugh
bellies joining in seesaws at your quick wit
I see her when you let yourself imagine
just for once

and fill a fresco with jeweled hues
telling legends of Shanghai and leopards
because you have always had
a beautiful way
with sketching tales
letting those tall, wild things climb
and I see her when you place
every piece of passed-down lace
every porcelain cream of pride
spinning light just-so
and I wish you could see
that you don't have to paint over
a prince's honest crown
that he never took
your legend could be a jeweled work of art
just on its own
tall, wild climb.

I UNDERSTAND DEEP LOVE HAS LEGS

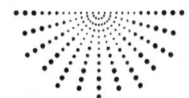

When I was five, my brother tripped me
while I was mid-pirouette
dancing at Disney World
pretending I was a mermaid
fluttering already
when I still had baby teeth
picturing arms swimming in an airy sea
and my brother couldn't resist
putting his legs out over and over
until like a whack-a-mole
boom he got one
young lips turning the color of
the little mermaid's hair dancing
into Florida's 'it's a small world after all'
streets now humming with
a five year-old's blood and joy
sprawling like ruby seaweed.

At the time, I felt so betrayed
and I remember my mother shouting
angry at my brother in Spanish
which is her highest decibel
of fury speaking
screaming for ice
and for years I wondered
why my brother felt that me
dancing imagination with curls
was such an unforgivable affront to him
that his legs whacked my mermaid tail.
I think he felt I was giddy
just to spite him
and so often I realize how
we create story whales bellowing
that might have only been bubbles
had we not drawn on them
fins and carnivore teeth
and even now I wonder
if that's what I'm doing
as I look back and try to paint reason
in tails and waves hovering above water
playing detective
Sherlock at Disney World
in my mind's eye
for why something that was just for me
my own inner world bouncing
could translate so sharply off key
to someone I've never not loved?

Yet as soon as the ice soothes the
swollen lip busted open

THE ONES THAT MADE THEIR MARK

inner world swimming scarlet and tender
I know that I can't help searching
for those underwater fish
the kind that know
how to make their own light
at the inky sea bottom
and every time my brother trips me
I take off my tail
try to hide its obnoxious shimmer
not give him reason to feel whale's teeth
and realize when it's just the two of us
away from the bubbles, the sea noises,
the cacophony of plastic
that seems to accidentally tangle up
in dolphin noses
I see two pairs of grown human legs
that never were blessed as natural hikers
and yet would walk through
dancing forests loud
with autumn's heartbeat
if the other ever sent a flame signal
blazing so scattered-orange into the sky
the rest of the din would slip elixir
to the fathomless depths
and the busted lips
the ice, the screaming
it gets forgotten in simmering
whirlpools of time
because the same legs that trip
have walked proud, have treaded lightly
to seek
to offer tender help

and love sometimes
it can bellow like a wounded whale
that as long as the fisherman don't fish
leave their boats on holiday
that as long as mermaids learn
the bait was never really meant for them
so bite for it less
a profound love can be
a brother who knows exactly how
to press the buttons only he understands
a brother who knows when to put
the carnivore away
and sprout legs to walk
and meet you on land
seasons and 'small worlds after all' more.

SHE SAID 'YOU CAN PAY US AFTER IT'S OVER'

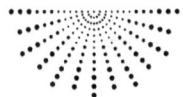

I tried hard on Zoom
I always try soft at heart
your friends made me cry

AULD LANG SYNE

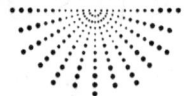

I've known you forever
and will love you twice over
even if one day
you don't have the perfect cups.

I spend such time
thinking about times past
wondering what makes
a friend love with uncorked forever
and what makes a stranger high-hat
hold disdain with pinky up
twice over.

Take the girl
who's so proud
that she's the one who knows
where to find the good cups,
the fun straws

for your party.
The one who brags that she knows
you have a new crepe maker
and you can't wait to make
Parisian treats delicious.

I think of what makes her
treat me with nose-up contempt
something I can feel
snappy through Zoom
and how she has no idea
the crepe maker
she's using as conversation currency
is a gift chosen with love
forever twice over
from me.

OH BLESS YOUR KANGAROO HEART

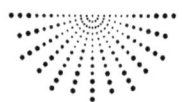

Did you grow up in a house
that sang three stories tall
where a library of laughter
seemed to hold the roof
big and wonderful
over your curious mind?

It's so strange to me
that we both have someone
so fair-haired to us
someone inseparable in common
like a stretchy Venn diagram
winding round our best friend's love
to our root-and-branch separate arcs
and still don't know each other
at all;
not a footnote in a story,
not a curiosity hanging onto a question,

THE ONES THAT MADE THEIR MARK

not a wobbling shingle on an old roof
big and wonderful
for all these years.

The funny thing is
I'd heard some of your stories
and I would have warmed to you
as if our roots and branches
had shared aurora in the sky
like yolk feeding the earth
big and wonderful
curious to find out the other home
that offered our dear friend
a library of hair-tossing laughter
something swimming steady
a roof for safekeeping
through those days of finding.

How could her grand pal
that legend has it
shared comfort like a life vest
be the same hollow stranger
that let me down?

I couldn't go to the party
big and wonderful as I hope it will be
but still I offered dollars
to entrust to you
a search to connect
to feel like a footnote in a memory
an outside shingle
pocket-sized in the house of new stories

I'm proud to see her building
like she's finally found it
the yolk of laughter's brightest
cooked up in the El Dorado sun.

All but three of you
acted like my money
whispered of cholera
and I got off that virtual call
feeling small and awful
so far from you
the you I'd thought I'd adore
through her bullion stories
reality sure lopsided those expectations
like a smashed orange
flattened into a peel
squandered juice, no edges
and somehow that felt
far from her
like you wanted to push me out
of a Venn diagram
something we've braided
like each other's laughing hair,
mind you-
long before you brought
your side of things onto her grid.

When you came back
with that in-your-face email
'You wanted to contribute something!'
well, you said, *now's your chance*
I was reminded of all those years

THE ONES THAT MADE THEIR MARK

she and I played in a house of pretend
big and wonderful
where through the fun,
we also learned to grow up
carrying a house full of honey stories
with us
the ones we imagined flowered up;
somehow it appears
like poison ivy mottling
the digital universe spanning
between us
talking Bloody Marys and themed fedoras
leaving me wondering why
the stakes feel so high
I catch it
unfog my wounded pride to see
you might have missed a weed
somewhere along the way
as if you learned two velvet blooms
must duel to share the sun;
if it wasn't so rotten,
I might feel sorrier for you
the vulnerabilities that are clearly
going popcorn-petty and wild
as the days unbraid
inching closer towards the festival
you just don't know me
how my leaves can breathe
just fine
without drinking your blaze
I'm not here to ruffle too much spotlight.

I wanted to stir up some magic
take you back through your memory
and let you see how for a day
you outright crumbled some shingles
off my roof
that would have been tall enough
to share
like the dollars you're right
I sure did offer.

The henchwoman who sassed
'*You can pay us after*'
is a curiosity you didn't bring up
in your cordial email
playing nice when the budget broke
and it isn't my place
to pose the question begging
to be asked here:
Was your library full of
dusty encyclopedias unopened
laughter shelved just too high
that you have the audacity
to come back for my generosity
with a kangaroo heart
bouncing from here to
your charmed circle's
one-blink town?

I hope you remember me
as you hammer out your roof
looking over with jealousy
at these honey bricks

THE ONES THAT MADE THEIR MARK

that you can't rid
from her Venn Diagram
that has us both circled to her;
I hope you blinked twice
when you read my response
the one where I took those dollars
back to my heart
all three stories tall.

FINDING THE CIRCLE

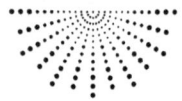

My father used to sing
walking in shuffled loafers
worn with happiness around the house,
'All my life's a circle, sunrise and sundown,'
and though my mother
tends to make up her own lyrics
even when the chords sounded different
they somehow sang together
all the same.

I think of how my brother and I
would sing The Lion King soundtrack
like we were antelopes lifting
'The Circle of Life!!'
chords that moved me
chords that made sense to me
even when I was young in the circle
I felt that even when my brother and I

THE ONES THAT MADE THEIR MARK

would wear happiness differently
we were also the same
and I loved being in his circle-
I still do.

I think of how my aunts and uncles
my cousins scattered across the U.S.
don't share the same lines
we so often wear the world differently
we don't always see things eye to eye
we sing the chords to lyrics written
in separate rhythms
but when life's sundowns strike
I know there's not a single sunrise
that wouldn't move us
to wear love's shuffled loafers
and walk to the gait of life's circle
not the same, but not alone either
and these are the chords
that move me now.

I think of how an accident
led me to change my story
how in the walk of leaving
I found first love
and though that love's circle shivered
and wore down
wearing the noose of life's shadow breath
it was at the end of my rope
I learned to wear heartache like a scarf
it's the end of my rope
that formed a new circle

where I met Rachel
my angel best friend
even though today she sings with halo
I hear her chords
they move me all the same.

I think of how Rachel had the love in her
to open up her circle
to a stranger like me
that from one line to the next
strangers entwine
in friendship extraordinary
in moments that shape our gait
as we walk shuffling loafers in time
cause to wear happiness around the house
cause to wear grief like a noose
that when we go far enough
through the circle
somewhere somehow we learn how
to wear it like heartache's scarf.

I think of the gifts she passed along
freely and fully
unafraid to make her circle bigger
because she had such love
no matter how we all wore happiness
how she gifted me her best friend
who as time circled
became my own
and introduced me to her circle
suddenly a trio of best friends
where I found sunrises I'd dreamed to feel

THE ONES THAT MADE THEIR MARK

because the circles when full
link up like candy necklaces
that we used to try on
in elementary school days
circles were bigger then
back when we only wore sweet sunrises
learning that kinship can link us
delight in the sharing, the passing along
as much as in the wearing
we'd eat the circles
candies on our tongues
all the same kaleidoscope
when we're young
our mouths are just circles
pinks turned reds by our necklaces
not so different.

I think of the twin I found
because we both love hummus and adventure
on our trip to Israel
how life's circle guided us to meet
and wear happiness over plates of shakshuka
and how she tells me
that she feels she knows a piece of Rachel
through me
like I passed along Rachel's candy necklace
just as she'd have wanted
and I think of the friends that fill my circle
how they've taught me to wear happiness
differently through life's changing loafers
and even when we're all making up the lyrics
as we go along

I feel the circle that builds us
new in sunrise
a chorus of us through sundown
life and loss ripple
and my father's song moves me
though the chords mean something different
I love them all the same.

CHAPTER 2

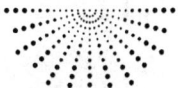

THE LUST BEFORE LIGHTNING

WE RUN OUR HANDS ACROSS THE CONTINENTS

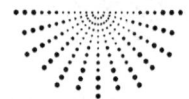

I'm a prize sap
sucked up from a tall ruby
maple tree roots roll below
tongue-deep as sugar:
Just one look
at his clean blue-gray
eyes could
make me boil
over.

Something
about the way
he carries himself so
smoothly- he just feels
every bit like
what a coiled Shabbat
challah *dream* should-
Oiled and glazed,

THE ONES THAT MADE THEIR MARK

a cross between
hand-made black leather jacket
and the crisp pages
of a favorite book
I want to pour over
and over.

I'm magma with him.
He's parched.
We ruin each other-
We rise frosted and sleek
out of the sleeping ashes.
Smoldering,
we run our hands
across the continents crossed
in our muscles.
I leave everything behind
creased satin cotton, traces of
him still in my tousled
lilac bed sheets.
I breathe him in
like that first beer I let
dribble on my tongue,
frothy and Israeli.

Somehow every new chapter,
I wind my way back
to him.
Swirling in marmalade dawn
rising from frozen fresh
plums with the Hot Israeli,
his skin a curtain of rainfall

hugging my tangled
boomerang heart
in the blushing space between
too late and ever-early-
I see just how
transformed I am
each *click*
of the Middle Eastern sands,
the dance we share
sugarmaker and plum hands
coastlines chasing dunes to
high-flying horizons almost flowing:
Back and forth,
the aftershave of sun-dipped skin
and lavender yearning that finds its sail
how we ripple in time
built like castles on the sand
made mortal with the tide of wavering
bend of touch, being touched,
the untold magic I keep glimmered secret:
bones I didn't know existed tingling, touching him
breathing out all of this like Pittsburgh rare
taken by shock-waves,
whenever he returns.

CHECKMATE: THE SEA-OF-FLAMES PROM KING

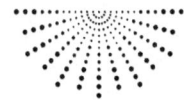

Pour out a live wire night
of green gin anticipation
with that oomph of intoxicated
peppery haze-
That's where I played
tug-of-war at the bar.
I vied for your whistling sea eyes
and even though I swore
I wouldn't compete
not with every international gaze
tossing wishes at your Romeo shoulders
I remember thinking,
but if I was, I think I'm winning
and at that point,
I wasn't about to back down
from the aphrodisiacal fight.

For jolting you

for midnight-misting me up
maybe for us both
maybe I just dipped into
Israel's intangible yearning
at all the right angles
how it bounced zesty
off your Amazonian grin
I stood ambitious on bar tops
that night on Dizengoff
the first cherrybomb afterglow
kissing like
Molotov cocktails
after months of breathless wanting
diagonal seats away in our program
how I wanted you
like solar power
sparking me up heartbeat-side out
beyond gravity
how I tried to pretend not to
and could barely convince myself
of the overbold laser lie
bouncing off mirrors
pulse riding to the moon
my bottle-green dress
dancing pendulum hip to hip
seeking yours
a hint of dark lace peeking
megawatts and melting heartbeats
a long way from Bardstown Road
this faithful Kentucky bookworm
in a new soda water time
moment of liquered truth giving off bubbles

THE ONES THAT MADE THEIR MARK

edging around the glass
I felt that girl leaving old book pages behind
putting vintage rules down
trading them in for an irresistible king
exposed
all for the international chance to play
a carbonated round of coquettish chess
crossing the mean girl rooks
who somehow all feel the same size
move across alike
on any side of the board
on any side of the world
only on this side of shifting pieces and captures
I melon-taste it
in the center of the bar
close to where
Habima Square flowers rise red from squares
how here I claim even the most coveted
sea-of-flames Israeli prom king
and for a green desert flash
I became grandmaster of the game
a night of gin anticipation checkmate
where dawn wakes up fizzy-kissed
juggernaut-awed
gambling a bookworm's fidelity
I made my lime wheel move
knocked it all off the timebomb board
and riding laser-like to the moon
light years away from
Louisville roads and the bookworm that didn't
play
not like this

I slide my queen like a catalyst
diagonal no longer
feel past pages snap in an excited blaze
and I spark my fingertips around
your neck
belonging to the infinite sea
drunk on conductivity
the leading light
and years later I know
that untold heartbeat-side
hot with terawatt-hours ticking
making a glorious mess
crossing impossible squares
it felt *mine*.

FIRE AND SUGAR- AND THERE WAS YOU

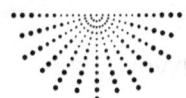

I pitched a hips hutch under a boy
who stripes himself as art disbeliever-
My unholy pursuit of skin-sticky easel
curling backbone distraction:
to smear over your bedroom eyes,
like Jackson Pollock on the run
from his splattered heart;
The artifacts we hide
explosive in chiseled trunks.

I had to try my escapist hand
at washing out
the drip thrill of our lips reveling
tasting polka dots
turning mouths redder,
plunge over
when you would draw in aura breath

banded exclamation
into your watercolor frame,
muzzle how you'd zip new notes
brimming through me
sandy-sweat swirls
Kentucky ankles and reckless siren
humming
in the witching hour.

I painted skin-drops under you again
to airbrush over a false lover
who knits his brows at the tang
of melted chocolate passion
and tears like a fever-scared rabbit
from a rustic magician's hat-
Intuition moves my thighs
right back to searching you.
I stir our cauldron
feel the flick of cheeks rocketing
defiant
and how you crave
my sun-butter brew.

You torched me, flying jaguar
hunting desert storm.
I basked in bourbon-smoking you wild-
My favorite sleight of Open Sesame.

It's a catch-22 now
without Monet's garden brush
dabbing dashes of palette

THE ONES THAT MADE THEIR MARK

pigment broken free
bristles turquoise alight
or eyelash spells
casting ultraviolet hooks
x-ray moments
the barest pair of jaws:
East-facing windows
sliding shoulder canvas
condensation on door sills
candlelight color bouncing
feeling awe, the all of you
understanding the whole of me
tasting the rebellious
confessions vibrating
ambrosia-inviting
city gleam falling
between us
starry night sinks beneath shores
as spontaneous as vivid sunrise,
jumbled blankets like thunder-
So much folklore held
in your slippery force-field
of temptation.

All of this casual
lacing under
puzzling over
when all I want is
caramel liberty
fire streaming
sparks set off between

jambalaya toes,
stunner sugar mixing
blueberry capillaries bewitched-
and a curious man like you.
Even when the bittersweet hangover leaves
me empty wishes in the woods
lawless
faith kite loose in winds blowing south
a tear-jerker who knew you were trouble
(of course, I knew).

I brushed a marked line- I know, I know now;
your multi-hued brilliance
skin just electric
it absolutely rouges and shatters.

But suddenly it's your Mediterranean eyes
setting combustible match
to my loving mind,
as much again
as ever before.
Your pull-me-in-strong sea tide
palms memories
transfixed in steam
this lust of madcap wonder.
Still, I filled my marbles with tea dreams,
deep cinnamon.
I'm the one who added
the honeycomb wand,
trickling.
I stirred the porcelain spoon,
just to flash your reflection once

more.

I couldn't bring myself to watch this time
when I arched it, tumbling
out the sea-scape window.
Is it under me now?

THE LAST THOUGHT I SPILL ON YOU

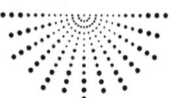

Moments we borrowed together
line in threads
baked into my pillow case.
Creased and crinkled.
Sesame seeds stitching
a Jerusalem bagel;
Rolled,
left to cool.

The cotton count raised,
levitating us-
like untied shoelaces
left perpendicular.
After each round of
freckled tic-tac-toe,
my curls
dipped into the Egyptian square,
marinated in you;

THE ONES THAT MADE THEIR MARK

Tel Aviv after sundown.

I remember your mountain chest
and my hitchhiker legs;
How between us,
we set free
runaway clouds of
manmade smoke.
Flushed
bodies in tune
melting
infatuation
atop
breathable fabric-
bedding that felt
so lush.
Ours
for lost hours
in passing
lifetimes.

My open heart tumbled,
rapture ungoverned
with this restless
Hercules,
Kentucky wildfire
in the Middle East.

Memories I wear like a forgotten crown.

Is this the year the Hot Israeli changed?
I see your face and I'm

off on a hitchhiker's prayer,
back where we began.
Threads and cases
cradle my moonstruck head-
But refuse rest
to my mind.

I can feel your touch,
your heat waning-
the memory of it
starting to flicker out;
Hanukkah candle sticks
finally melt down their last
bit of oil.

And maybe that's the miracle-
The way my heart
boils over
your blue eyes.
The way candles
take the chill off
borrowed beeswax.

SET A MATCH

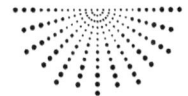

Just call my curiosity
this flickering candle.
The tiny flame
bats like teasing eyelashes
mid-bluff
behind the cocktail glass,
gorgeous lime raining mist.
Wink, blink twice.
I re-apply *Summer Nights*
gloss catchy on my lips
play its bar glow
like this store-bought sun
is my unbeaten ace.

The candle flutter keeps winking-
practically daring me
across my second toast
a cheers to the night life

served crowd-pleasing
in a flower-tipped martini glass
photosynthesis in my green hands.
I sip the evening, delicately
restraining all the roar
of a fire tigress.
I fog up
every ridge of untouched cosmos.
I growl in candle purrs.

FLIRTING 88 DAYS 'ROUND THE SUN

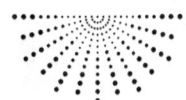

Fresh out of the army,
his marble arms wake me alive-
Like a coffee pot switched on,
brewing spiced new romance.

He takes me by surprise
on a hot tin roof
mid-February-
our bated breath
imploding origami.
I feel him tipsy with the confidence
of halcyon days.
I can kiss it on those
blush-pink
memory foam lips.

On back
of whispered touch,

the Young Israeli carries me
to Budapest hot springs:
Provocative.
It's as if he knows the mystery.
How the warmth
separates
the cool snap of the
Danube air,
in two.

Glass steam on marble,
he's teaching me-
That velveteen rainwater
can spread like
honey-touched milk on my tongue.

Maybe it's his moonwalker's smile
shaking me up.
He's a high-rise,
a tall glass of frothy ocean waves-
A Kentucky girl's head turner,
and my favorite fool's paradise.
I drink him right up.

The Young Israeli
makes his way through
the softest pools of satin-
He sweeps me in
with the calm strength of underwater
heartbeats,
hot jets swooshing,
lapping up all my wishes;

turning them inside out.

When I'm right side up,
I'm his cherry red
sugar high from Mercury
after flirting 88 days 'round the sun.

That's when age flips,
a seaboard handstand,
a flotsam sum
drowned out-
I can't see anything else
but the Saturn rings
caught spinning,
racing in his eyes.
Or am I seeing
the reflect of
galaxies ladled
into mine?

I rise and fall
with each dreamy odyssey breath-
His solar power
empire
bowing at sunset.

I LIKE TO CALL HIM '007

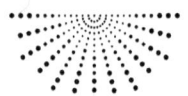

The young hot Israeli has many
names in my mind.
He calls himself *"Hiking Boots."*

I can call his James Bond touch
anything
but I have no doubt: it's not mine
as he turns desert boots into socks
into toes without a stitch
I wonder
who else has seen them
upside down.

I'll joke and tell my girls
"I just joined a new gym on Levinski."
"It's a good thing you're getting
that membership for free," says Chloe.

THE ONES THAT MADE THEIR MARK

It's a gym with floating hours
and a young Israeli
changing shoes
laces cartwheeling
across the bedroom floor
but I know he's not making dates
I know that's not this hiker's style.

"You can rename me now," he says.

We glow-
Our bodies in blacklight
an exhilarating rush of rodeo.
Our bodies engraving beds,
a jungle gym dance in mirrors.
I've never seen and starred
in such a show.

"You gave a dull day color," he whispers.
Why does my brightness
his whisper
feel lost to hypersonic Tel Aviv
once again
and how can I hold on to it all
to this
the jungle colors glowing between his skin
and what's mine
gripping these pull up bars
flipping, bending, contorting 360 degrees
how to keep the mirrored days and nights of us
in technicolor that won't run
in another wash of starlight sighs?

Even if I try
to close my gym membership
hours like fiction I dreamed up
how can I quit the undressed fantasy
how does '007's neck
somehow bottle
a forest's tree leaves
after the rain, sweating
oak and vanilla
intoxicating
maple sap droplets?
It feels so good it's almost imaginary.

But I can so clearly
breathe the passion in like sweet smoke
glistening
practically steaming
hot off his dewy body-
And so I'll come clean:
I find myself, windswept
by a pair of boots undone
a sucker for those eyes like big blue marble
nectar lips forever
leaving mine candy-coated.

Do you think I'm queen of this hive
or willingly caught
in the young Israeli's honey jungle?
Either way, here I simmer
covetous,
craving

THE ONES THAT MADE THEIR MARK

aglow-
Fit for a fresh king
who likes the way I feel
like I'm straddling in technicolor.

LETTER TO MY 13 YEAR-OLD SELF

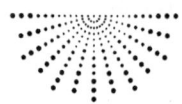

Dear Young J,

Never pick the guy who's
"good on paper."
He'll plant a seedless kiss,
and all you'll taste is
water streams gone missing
in the dead of night;
just like this
suitor from Fluency Israel
who has not one, but two framed
signs to convince
second-guessers
just how cloying
"home-sweet-home" really is.

I look back:
Was this boy

THE ONES THAT MADE THEIR MARK

an amorous hopeful
mind-surfing the crowd
in a nautical striped polo, or
a campaigner for fireside politics?
An on-the-make
abstract lover
penciling
plans in
nucleus strings,
like he's skipping the line
at TSA check for valentines.

He must think apricot sparks
course between
hearts,
solidify like clay:
Does he ever find out
we can't go fish
for lovers as if
tumbling down
chimney corners?

Look up: a poster
forging "love" is misspelled,
an ersatz heart of hearts
haywire in French no less.

When he invites us back for tea,
you and I-
the blissed out teen I carry
that tickles my lungs like
tangerine anemone-

well- *we*
tend to swim with the tide, longing
to feel infused:
We've set our wants on
a warm Juliet cardamom that
fills Romeo teacups
full with
chai in heat,
brown sugar and black
peppercorn-zesty;
Spicier by the minute
the mix gives into the warm-up.

How you've felt that pining
like hopeless romantic tie-dye
staining your rib cage
with the pull of
anticipation.
It's what you document
without words
when you crush on a
beautiful hazel blue-eyed boy
who's busy trying to throw
shadow monsters off his neck.
His untried love simmers
like a London tea
blowing a soft invisible kiss
through sterling fog.
Undiluted,
the real McCoy;
Only forever a sip
out of our touch.

THE ONES THAT MADE THEIR MARK

So real even as children,
his aches could cry
hazel-blue onto
loose-leaf paper.

But here's what
I wish I could slip into
your Lisa Frank-stickered
notebook, holographic and bright,
like a Dame Fortune in twinkling
emerald, speaking a world to come:
The ones who are good on paper
will never come close to
a kettle catching its breath.

The ones who aren't,
and all the shadow monsters
dogging after-
Aren't yours to hold.

Though every so often,
I catch your fleecy hope
tender that those shadow monsters
sleep-walk on moon-stirred axis-
That the ones quiet and searching
open coconut truth-gates
on their way home.
But that's a chamomile prayer,
I remind you:
Not a pebble soft as night sky
to guard in fingertips, with gem-lit trust.

Bit by bit, it's *us*
you're crossing fingers for,
wishing on Jaffa's Wishing Bridge,
lusting after
like halo blooming high tea.

Together, you and I infuse
an iron-willed
kettle whistling sparks,
cardamom hearts up, afloat,
thoughts brave as Masala
washing hot water.

Without,
all we hold is a stray cat's purr,
a lion's mirage
that won't shake the dead
in the palms of our
wonder-thirsty hands.

This suitor can only
try on a
Ginsberg-howl for size.
You'll see it too,
when you hear the posters
he left up
from the young tenants
who poured tea
before him.
They aren't even his.

His jello love will

THE ONES THAT MADE THEIR MARK

no more imbue ours
than two frames can
bring us "home sweet home."

All we're left with is
a *never-howl*
that's starting to look
a hell of a whole lot less
good on paper.

YOGURT

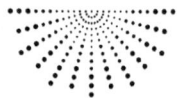

I see it three years later
your neck tightens like a stopwatch
the curdled way you see me
I just know you must
remember my words
the art of war
the worst ones I ever pieced
I loaded those parting shots to linger
and I see they've lasted
like that 405 year-old clam I read about
in National Geographic
you've become an above water arrowtooth eel
twisting and quaking
the stubborn sting of electric vengeance
when I find you again
in the new office kitchen
I had clean forgotten
all about you

your selfish pride
it's almost funny how it clings
the same way the kiss of spider webs do
shivering, sticky netting
still smoking pockmarks under your chin.

I forget it's you until I see your neck
how the veins snake in panic
how that exquisite pinch of tension
carries beetroot pride
the one I bruised three years ago
a Sisyphus stone you had tossed aside
now hanging heavy
a busted talisman
existentialist dread taut around your neck
the world doesn't see any of this but I do
I have the kind of sensitive sight that *sees*
the extraordinary and the grotty
I could turn it either lovable or detestable
and when I kissed you by the Jaffa sea
how it shot up in a delicious Ursula roar
after we ate at the restaurant called Blackout
I didn't see the brittle in you yet
excited with the curious sea misting around us
I could see the sales lady wishing me
luck on the date with you, my gentleman caller
when I bought a new Italian scarf in Tel Aviv
except now
I see it's something you wouldn't notice
how I chose "surprise me" on the menu
wanting every dish to be
simmering adventure.

I wish I had seen it then
before surprised eyes
because my face could tell
my skin must have cast a hex
protecting against your demons
when my tender chin rejected you
a scarred rash from ignoring your roughness
so simmering for adventure
I turned blind sight to your stubble like hooks
lost in the tangle of faces misting adventure
I lied and told my brother that I had tripped
drunk walking into my apartment
something believable
bandaging the pyramids of scrapes rising
the Mesa mean girls laughing at me
'Julie what happened to your FACE?'
and all I'm thinking is *you*
you happened to my face
as I hung my head getting ice cream
your grotesque branding my chin
an awful you-shaped scarlet letter
all this before my heart and mind ever
caught on
reached for the ammunition
thinking just this once I'd unleash
my most scathing
try on for satisfying size
since my friends know
you wouldn't even know
where to find the atlas
how to satisfy a simmering woman like me
the temptation trembled

THE ONES THAT MADE THEIR MARK

how it might feel to obliterate a scoundrel
if I at last let myself off the hook of "good"
and I used my words like a howitzer
thinking the next time I'd see you was
second after never
so how was I to know
I couldn't have read in any tea leaves
that one day I'd be stonewalled
right by the plastic forks
in a clumsy boa constrictor
bolt from the blue.

I call dates like you "yogurt"
because you start off real sweet
but you curdle sour in the fridge
and three or four weeks later
into the trash you go
because there's nothing worth
even recycling here.
That's what you were:
a yogurt that spoiled so loud
it shocked me to see the sour gurgle
first week on the new job
having just fled Wall Street cockroaches
much bigger than you.

I knew it was you by your neck
because it scrunched up just as before
like a reddening crab scuttling
when I'd later try to describe it
it felt like hungering
for movie theater popcorn

only to dip my hands and find out
the paper carton is full of all butter
and kernels that didn't pop
it all happened so quickly
I didn't even know the kernels
were detectable to the human touch
when you pulled out like a Chevy
after a screech and run
barely there on the hit
bulldozer on the run
starched collar buttoned up
when I came back from the bathroom
thinking
well everyone has off days let's try
let's try this again
shake the nerves out like kernel duds
and I saw you there
belt snapped like a train's cogs clicking
realizing you could care less
about anyone but your own damn gluttony
your chin like a perfect alibi
offering to order me a taxi
a taxi I'd have to pay for
as long as you could keep the app's points
and I sure thought you had
some masterful audacity
for a boy who came up short
on popcorn satisfaction
all butter no pops
and made me bring the wine.

"If you wanted it to be about fun

THE ONES THAT MADE THEIR MARK

you should have made it more fun…"
I felt so angry texting you that
feeling the sass of being fresh to Israel
having waited so long before
trying someone new
and there came along your blowfish lips
your face like some kind of
American poison ivy
I surrendered to walking home indignant
by the Central Bus Station at midnight
before I'd surrender my pride to you too
or those taxi points
that couldn't have been that important
and you prioritized the nothingness
all the same
aggravated because I should have seen
the dreary close-up and personal
but chose to see the extraordinary
when really what was buttered up
was the Ursula sea
the Italian scarf dancing in Tel Aviv
exotic thrill around my neck
just waiting for you to untie it
the simmering adventure around us
only to be served an empty plate cold
you walking away like
the wolf ate Little Red whole
thinking you'd get away with it
as you'd been working in Israel
longer than I had
fancy apartment and a beautiful dog
and there I come back

Ghost of Women You Didn't Satisfy
to haunt you scarlet in
the worst "surprise me" place possible
the office kitchen
because up until now
you felt this was all yours
and I see you look like
you've got lettuce stuck in your teeth
as the pride wraps around your neck
American horror story
tight lobster heart mid-business meeting
witnessing I've truly arrived
the girl you screwed over
without screwing well
guess what she's in the same office kitchen
surprise
and you didn't read me right
I can see that now
but I sure love a good one
the way *surprise* sounds like a glorious slither
it crackles like popcorn in my body
the way you never could
because I know you didn't expect me to stay
as long as my words clearly did.

I come back to my desk
boiled potato uncooked
remembering this reminder
of unpopped popcorn
it's got to be worse for you
than the
I can believe it's not butter

THE ONES THAT MADE THEIR MARK

blink-and-you'll-miss-it
satisfaction was
bending back three years ago
for me
when I spelled it out for you
and hit *send*
now feeling like a feisty tiger at work
an American in hi-tech Tel Aviv
because you didn't see it
I'm the girl who stays and satisfies
and I got my stripes and sight back
neck smooth and leisured
as yours is tight with cold sweat
the surprise you didn't choose
but you made your bed
and three years later
trick or treat, Yogurt
you find yourself lying in it
I'm the red quivering knots around your neck
as I think of the
movie theater feasts
that sure have hit the spot
I've relished ever since.

I'M NOT YOUR CHINA DOLL

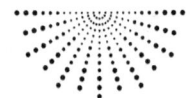

When the eye rollers aren't
setting me aside
thinking all I am is
a teaspoon of vanilla
this girl's a funny dash of wholesome
a one-note happy under their noses
eyebrows like tents and glass houses
as I walk like a magic trick beneath
a sea universe of colors up my sleeves,
if italics expressions could talk
I find it too easy to steal
those other sideways looks
that spell out-
Porcelain plaything.

Oh don't
give yourself so much credit
thinking your italics smile

THE ONES THAT MADE THEIR MARK

is written in bold.
I've yet to meet a man
who didn't think he was
a one-of-a-kind bull
in my fragile little china shop.

I'm nobody's dollface
but a glassy choir of eyes
that don't see me when they look at me
seem to lay claim
that my sleeves and walks of colors
belong to their "dream girl."

"You're just so my type,"
I've heard them drawl
disco ball echoes down an empty well
to the point it feels almost lazy
watching myself
foreign and see-through
fuzzy resolution in their idealizing eyes-
just a sweet thing, a real pin-up.
A telescope doll centerfold,
tallest on the crystal shelf
so high, no living wonder can reach.

In your newsstand ears
you see my painted mouth
quiet as an orchid
unless I'm calling you **Handsome**
like a read-all-about-it headline-
But hear me when I say, *darling*,
you're not my idea of dreamboat

any more than I'm your angel trinket
a halo wrapped around your mind.

I'm a hot dish of starburst
just out, hot-to-touch
whether they see it or not
the wilderness in me tingles
open-air spicy
like leopard-signed old waboom trees
and you're so busy
starving to see you in me
you can't hear mother nature
dancing deja vu with me
between your syllables-
already *breaking*
your bargain basement glass.

I LOVE A GOOD RED FLAG

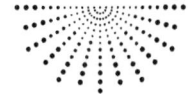

Don't mind me
just wearing my shade of trouble
waving Jessica Rabbit mischief
taking the wind on as my dress
to drape it bright around my hips.
It's a siren's wink-
when I kiss it on my lips,
in a pool of rubies
like gemstones rippling
setting the compass in my smile.
I suddenly know
exactly how to
cross every respectable line
as easily as skin softening butter
with a single fabled touch.

Time saunters reckless
in a pair of strong hands chasing seconds

across a ticking clock
with a face that looks like mine
when I'm done waiting
like how I wind my own strings
sent quivering with the sound
of raw anticipation
there's nothing complicated about
these instincts
each deep-toned bell
ballooning
just as Time watches
my inner femme fatale
get tied up
in wild and stormy knots
like my brain's wise unzips
buttons and wits needing a seamstress
scattered like handwritten letters
paper-mache to the floor.
It's a downright torrid
tale as old as many a tango-
going for the seductive island boy
that disappears into famous myth.

I'm not one to turn down
this rhythm of musical chairs
cut loose
sometimes the *shouldn'ts* feel inviting
maybe it's that they're lighthearted
an original mural
cherry tongues and *baby's* and bar glasses
clapping tangled against walls
how a seascape detour

THE ONES THAT MADE THEIR MARK

becomes a simple reprise
sweet and sour
flags away from the traffic of longer days
I get distracted
bored to playdough tears
because these so-called "nice guys"
text me on apps
but I know they're imitators
pretending to be hopefuls
the kind folks of the world
don't tend to walk around with a sticker
sharpie ink loudly sharing
"HEY MY NAME IS *NICE*"
good souls just are
they exist without all this shouting about
it's not this dull thud of
"My contribution is my distinction
can't you see how virtuous I am?
Look at me donating to you now
like you're my new favorite charity"
these copycats talk stale about dentist appointments
looking for a receptacle for every thought
without any more interest in my own
than the dates wrapping red flags around me
as if they just want to click *play* on
sitcom entertainment
laugh track ready
it's like scooping out
molasses remnants stuck
at the bottom of a mason jar
static
lukewarm at best;

They expect my stirrer to put on a show
as a clever enough statue
made silver to marvel at the goings on
of slow-moving molasses
perpendicular and wowed up.

So Time sees me
spinning far from run-on sentences
from tangos to the laps of chairs
craving capital letters
even if they sometimes bend
because they're not the nicest
I like that they're vivid
three-dimensional
live-out-loud messes
no post-its or pretenses.

Time will tell you
I draw a breath
rubies and compass
into each saucy night
where urban myth says
I reapply that dynamite red
on Bourbon Trails to islands
vagabond lips blowing kisses at danger.
I don't tell the pretenders
until my turpentine curls go up in smoke:
I'm devoted only to matching
the shade of my favorite warning.

TRY SAYING NO IN ITALIAN

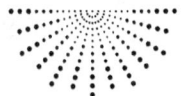

The universe is testing me
presenting the beautiful, beautiful Italian
and his strong jaw line
as rugged and stalwart as
Old Rome.

As I sit beside him
this restaurant evening,
I'd wish on a wine satellite
for him to draw my savvy
outside of myself
spirits dreamland-bound
where wisdom wafts
like moon dust into pitaya instincts
sweet serendipity-
he has no idea
how resisting is
taking one look at the Italian pools

dripping amaretto-honey
Giovanni calls *eyes*
as I feel my body rising
to take flight
and managing to stay put.

This is not my match
there's a beauty that isn't quite catching
he's not leading
my soul up the garden path
so why does walking home
still feel like oil warming on a stove
when I know this fascination is just
sunlit-speckled dust
swirling in a sidelined room?
Soccer-set frame,
this muscled daytripper lights up Tel Aviv
Italian sauces bubbling by the sea;
but deep in my heart
that lightning-strike
kindred bond
the great mystery that keeps my intuition
ever-searching
time zones and map grids
my soul when it curls like pasta
freshly cooked around a fork
I know isn't playing violins here
on city streets where we share goodwill
but our conversation doesn't sing
we're not vibing divine.

I want to tell him

THE ONES THAT MADE THEIR MARK

I'm not looking for a new grease fire
because I remember what happens
I've left one too many delicious
pans unattended
on a hungry stove
my tenderness needed aloe
and they don't sell that kind
you can't buy back heartache seconds;
the truth pangs past longing
setting in my eyes like the desert winter sun
that no matter how many moments
I search to find the night in him
my mind can't shake it
the sea can't pull the moon
even when picturing that glow
swimming orchestras
dancing through glass waters.

Oh, the absolute defiance it takes-
to want *more*
to say, "It was a pleasure to meet you, Giovanni"
the kindest farewell I've ever known
as we wave a goodnight goodbye;
to learn to only just begin saying: no.

DESERT ATLANTIS

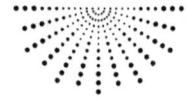

Deep copper eyes flashed
like sky lanterns
defying gravity in the Negev desert
buttering me up like
richly honeyed bread
upturning in the oven.
Malik was silver-tongued,
luscious as pear nectar,
sweeping me off my feet
before I had barely stepped
jean-jacket-off the plane in Eilat.
Fresh-faced, striped luggage in tow,
I wandered into the sunglasses shop.
A sleek pair of Dior's
catching my attention first
and then,
there was Malik.
Strong like an olive tree,

THE ONES THAT MADE THEIR MARK

tattoos wrapping around his arms like
moonless black vines.
With those same tanned hands
he would later
pop my cyclone breath
as if opening champagne bottles-
I made him *desert-thirsty*;
Firewater brewed for guzzling.

I could tell
read it in the ivy
living in his eyes
roots beckoning back to Lebanon-
I was a cannonball gulp of new
Kentucky air rousing
sighing
through the routine of paradise;
but so was Malik for me.
There's just something about
a holiday turn of mind
that calls forth the
devil-may-care wanders
carried quiet at heart
spurs the silver-tongued lightning rod
rebel Eve in me.

I indulge in an escapade
like I'm willing to dare wisdom
luscious through my teeth,
kicking up my heels higher than garden gates,
a smoking relisher of the riot.
I'm sure the mere thought

would have sent some family reeling
so I tucked all the silver and fruits I could carry
like a message in a bottle
hidden in the heartbeats
writing glow-lamp melodies
like a pair of paradise lips
blurred against skin
ticking trees of sudden knowledge
above my belly button
almost whole apples suspended in time.

By the go-that-a-way
lull of Red Sea waves
our only audience as we tiptoed on wet grass
outside the Isrotel Royal Garden,
we found a hush of body peace
strangers shimmering
into something hair-raising
that brilliant moment of becoming *more*-
Dipping our toes
awash in Atlantis
if only for a night.

AIR HEART

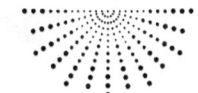

The Man o' the Jets had the lightest
Lantern eyes
He didn't torch me-
I felt illuminated
Like we were crossing street lights
Sending out flares to each other
Close and trembling fireflies
In the mist.

That first midnight,
He kissed my lips
Until they blossomed.
Blush pink hyacinths
Learning to open.

My eyes watered awake-
'This is teardrop travel,'
I thought.

This is what it means
To feel
Full of heart.
Like I had drawn in
That lantern-light whole.
And just like that,
He unbolted me.

In the beginning,
It felt like sweet new promises
As if we were finespun lace,
Gentle and within reach.

An Israeli with the greenest gaze
And me,
His Lady of the Four Roses.
'This is rare,' he sang.
The softest chords
Weaving lullabies.

The stars he scribbled
He'd ink in lantern-light
And my heart felt like it
Belonged.
Not to him- but to his walking beam.
The night he saved my purse
From beach thieves
I watched him reflect light-
My sandy-haired protector.
Naked bottle green eyes and
Umbrella kisses,
The Man o' the Jets'

THE ONES THAT MADE THEIR MARK

Shoulders were sea-worthy,
Navigating me true north.

But like Amelia Earheart-
My Man o' the Jets went missing
In his quest to 3D map the globe.
As if the light in him
Slivered through California cracks,
Vanished somewhere in the Redwood trees.
A heart part of him was lost to the sea
And the air
And jets that soared overseas,
Far away long after he returned.

I want to cling to forgotten breath
Of lantern-light.
But once he's mapped out new worlds
Without me
And I've felt lips blooming alive
All it feels is lost-at-sea.
It's teardrop travel
Turning cheeks steely.
The light's soggy now.

I tell him,
It's too dark to see here anymore.
He tells me he feels 'ominous.'
And I cry, I'm sorry- I'm chasing the
Light.

Now, I etch new maps,
Bury treasure,

And build and crash lighthouses
All over town.
Spring flooded into ominous December.
And I still can't help but wonder,
Did Amelia feel wayward and cast away?
Or is she just in hot pursuit
Of lost true north
Through naked green eyes?

PETER PAN TASTED LIKE JAZZ

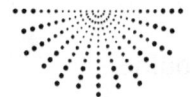

I met Peter Pan not in Hollywood town
where his laugh once made the moon fly
the brother of a vivacious girl
who told me
in the middle of the jazz scene
"You've *got* to meet my brother"
l'chaim! in New Orleans
spilling drinks with three kinds of liquor
sharing about the boys that came
hurricanes before the Land of Oz
drunk promises we'd made ourselves
the best kind
how next time would be different
next time we'd do right
by our cathedral hearts
we'd treat them like honest sanctuaries
and in walks Peter Pan
standing there flashing his outright

boyish charm
and all I can remember
is how I was caught
drink a loose magnet in my hand
caught in his larger-than-life LA charisma
the first tall Jewish boy to hook
my fresh captivation
standing there in a Grammy's tee
that hugged his square shoulders
swagger and charisma in cool glasses
a smile made to show it off
and I'm suddenly forgetting
that my first love had left me lovelorn
because there's Peter Pan
magnetizing me, my drink, the very energy
singing jazz from my fingertips
like if Lake Quilotoa
one of my favorite forever sights
with all its hypnotic turquoise
and its glassy violet
could hum in bold colors out loud
that first time we locked coffee eyes
getting cinematic in the bar
sounding like
it just might re-puzzle
the fractured hopeless romantic within.

The first love taught me
how many unknown angles my heart
could shatter like a mirror cracking
left me with the shards to figure out
how on earth to kintsugi them back together

with handmade gold
and with Tinkerbell fingers that stirred
the radiant glue
I'd learn how I could touch a new heart
and how his fingers might see the sanctuary
lifting up a prayer to melt pieces like watercolors
how with my second love
I'd take the second star to the right
happy thoughts astounding to Neverland
I'd discover my broken heart could feel love
for a time that would never grow old.

I dared myself to go to New Orleans
and then
when I met the prince of the lost boys
he didn't feel lost
he felt certain in a fantastical way
when my heart was low on pixie dust
and felt anything but certain
curious what love might feel like again
after my first love told me with crocodile teeth
I'd never know
so what a perfect place
to find out never *never* existed
in New Orleans kissing Neverland
where it felt audacious *not* to love Peter Pan
it's all I could do
to ask myself "What would Carrie Bradshaw do?"
away from familiarity
I let myself believe in him
pendulum pulled
and in doing so

I believed in second love's sanctuary
I believed Tinkerbell's handmade gold
could fix up a heart spilling three kinds of hope
as I believed beignets were dazzled
with Louisiana pixie dust
it was real
it was Lake Quilotoa melodies possible
as I wanted to taste beignets
singing jazz from his smile
made to turn Fantasia
duplicate that smile onto my face
two strangers turning lovers
making a movie in the jazz club
that played on til morning.

Kissing Neverland
I understand why Wendy believed
"Oh… it was such a wonderful adventure!"
because how I wished
to feel renewed space
rise in my loving broken heart
like wings for these cinema dreams untold
only to find a sanctuary silver screen in me
touched unbroken
such trust undusted with pixie beignets
a night's bottled up *astounding*
in Peter Pan's go-ahead smile
and there was that Wendy in me
believing
this state of grace will never grow old

Sometimes I can catch

THE ONES THAT MADE THEIR MARK

in a second love corner of
absinthe clouds
see my heart space shaped
like a wish
burrowing
into an eternity of new
I can savor it
way back when
where going away didn't mean forgetting
that playful shadow winking
crowing beautiful
forever for a jump
Hollywood town charisma to the dancing moon
flying straight on
the kind of love that heals in tastes
til morning dreams dawn
when a weekend
stretched wide as an appetite
lagoon songs fixing in my mind
Hollywood lifting Kentucky
star to the right high
New Orleans deep in Neverland
running rosebud tongues over
the pixie dust in our mouths
chests flushing cider wine
full of Fantasia attraction
cathedrals booming
handmade gold steady as
a pair of hot shadows
burn the midnight oil
all that once shattered
ringing together

unanimous
and I believe the nevers
are never quite so
like I adore the always
that sometimes gets lost
and when my heart
made something kintsugi new
plays the scene over again
in a nostalgic land
never nudging always
looking out the old window
from the Darling house
cinema glitters like strangers
24 karats flying full of jazz songs.

BEFORE YOU SHOUTED "FIRE!!!" IN HEIDELBERG

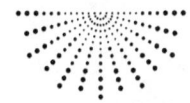

Your golden tongue spun
word alchemy
revving a wheel of colors
from the mirror of my mind
to yours
my Northern Lights stretching
Babel high
through the marvel
swinging those first messages on JSwipe
our hot nerve center
the dating app the Mesa girls had said
was for meeting boys who wanted real
relationships and not just laundry hookups
and because laundry had never spun
wonders for my mind
even though it's nice on skin
for a flint spark moment
I invested new career money

into fine lace lingerie
to criss-cross dazzle a man to his knees
moonlight I wanted suitors to feel
looking up
when my soft skin might kiss theirs alive
something touching deeper than laundry
an orbit that could turn a summer
to cinnamon garnet.

You made my mind excited
your thoughts touching brilliant
a train run past laundry chats
leaving "hey what's up?" in the rearview
you were never small talk and I loved that
so I gave you undivided attention
silk moving over my lungs
drawing breath through the air
cinnamon garnet revving
because it was charming how you wore
mismatched socks
and those dark New York scarves
talking poetry over pizza slices
you said they could almost rival your favorites
even if not quite
outside the light rail in Jerusalem.

Our first Shavuot together
the only one in our history
you introduced me to your neighbors
next door they made me feel right at home
shared a plate full of phenomenal
French cheese saved for the holiday

THE ONES THAT MADE THEIR MARK

still I felt embarrassed we met on an app
it somehow felt ordinary
didn't mirror in our minds
how we felt
how we talked in word alchemy
wheel of colors sparking flints
touching something brilliant
waking up slumbering magic
with tricks of our tongues
every witty volley taking me on a train
tracks of decadent homespun words
you made my mind excited in Jerusalem
eating up a plate of that jaw-dropping cheese
they'd been saving
for the right time
so generous with us.

I could swear by your plain English
as I sat next to you
feeling right at home
your left hand like calligraphy on my thigh
when you swung a circus beginning
the decoy story was a marvel
so we kept adding bones
unscripted
the costumed sentences jumping between us
growing elaborate shoots and stalks
we started talking clever in front of them
elephants and tightropes
swinging at the circus
our first three-ring secret
and maybe I liked burlesque imagination

more than reality with you.

We were flirtatious
head over heels
hot skin misty on the terrace
trying Turkish coffee
glasses steamed up too
sharing poetry that turned our fingers
messy navy with ink lacing us
even the silence we would share sometimes
touching something brilliant.

I loved the journey I took
just to get to Rashi Street
so many weekends I spent only at your place
north of the children's playground
I smiled open as I'd pass by
walking through Machane Yehuda
to turn at the admiral blue
painted face on the wall
hop on bus 485
to arrive tangled in the circus of you.

We read lilacs and turned stories in the fields
our beginning flushed in blackberry winter
I can find it again
trace memory's lace
asking Kinguisha what to wear
when hiking through spring
with a lover I thought
I could marry someday.

THE ONES THAT MADE THEIR MARK

Opening up old heart scars in Jachnun Bar
sneaking into a secret Purim party
underground
I entered that garage
a vampire full of Kentucky dreaming
Tel Aviv sangria-red on my lips
making my way through
solving the empty car park maze
the one your friends designed
they were impressed
I could figure it out
and still I know
all that mattered to me
through that first labyrinth
through cloaked underground secrets
was if it impressed you.

Trains I took for your admiration
it was all I set my tightrope-walking heart on
not seeing any elephants in the room yet
back then it was just champagne
shared in the closet
my Tel Aviv red like a coat of arms
trains traveling your New York cheeks
your Jerusalem neck
your North and my South surrendering
like cursive poems translated
50 years later
meanings good and stirring
historic in every new revision
bottles knocked over, bubbly icing the floor
brightening up my leather boots and I didn't mind

a country of frothy pearls beneath us
we were dreaming with our circus tongues awake.

The night I lost my costumed glove
we were at our beginning
saucy writers risking
hearts and word alchemy on the same page
translated in delicious symmetry
any champagne countries or gloves lost
that just felt like a train station revving
a promise of feeling new
when feet walk across railroad tracks
anything but shy
when stamping the world with soles
equal and opposite reaction
nothing felt forfeited then
it was the glove of a vampire
fantasy at stake
I'd take a train back through history
tell myself to notice the missing glove
lost imagination can be expensive
still, when there's a curious hand
to take its place
turn it lacy red with a rush through the
metacarpus ungloved
a glove lost in a maze gets overlooked
so we dined on cherry-picked words love
an autumnal equinox between minds.

The Shabbat evening I met your mother
I purchased flowers before
the hometown girl in me full of nerves

THE ONES THAT MADE THEIR MARK

restless on my lunch break
I thought my roommate was a creative genius
she warned me
about your mother
how your mother dismissed her in a blink
and that left me mighty uneasy
taut as elephants stamping my bones
I was full of nerves and in search of flowers
wandering my way to the bottom of the Shuk
I remember you said she'd appreciate that
you were so smart and so wrong
she never did.

She's the kind of person
who I doubt ever understands
a florist studying love
until the radiance of petals
stains her hands wise
your mother doesn't see below pedestals
there's honor in searching
handing over blossoms
that will go places
grow in the gifting
the florist is generous in the before
sharing pieces of her
kept in the back of the store
I feared your mother
in the before I didn't translate it
what must have been lost in a maze
long ago
I bet she hasn't felt
homespun feelings that turn conversations velvet

like how at first the florist didn't realize
that for Americans meeting the parents
that's a big deal, I explained
and so she handed me her best florals
a unique selection of plant kingdom
with the nice pot, she knew *just* the one
hopeful for a shidduch
a fiery American *match* in the holy land
she could see poetry was unlatched
deep in my skylight eyes
all that your mother wouldn't figure out
because some feelings are beyond books
and your mother I imagine
spends her train rides
looking down
on people like me.

There I floated
outside your family's building
you swung a painted gate
the color of a dusk sky speaking
before midnight
but what I really remember
is how my Kentucky matches struck sky
flints sparking a history inside my soul
with all that vigor and energy
the dance of the flicker
before flames stretch up
or get snuffed out.

Holding fresh flowers
that painted the florist's hands

THE ONES THAT MADE THEIR MARK

and now mine
I hoped your mother might love them anyway
even though I heard fair warning
I was hoping she might love me
such flickering circus hope that you might
one day love me
and I think of how my mom will often ask
why I want everyone to love me
I crave it
flowers growing roots into my palms
a history maze
I could spend my whole life
and the ones that came before
figuring out.

There I balanced in a scene of houses
it felt like standing in a gallery
Tel Aviv's historic first neighborhood
dangling on the mere thought
the first love I'd allowed this far
swinging into my heart
in so many falling stars
after many curls of sun
seen flickering from both hemispheres
seen snuffed out too
so when I met your mother
and she said Harry Potter was
the downfall of civilization
Waterloo as we knew it
I sat at that table
circus hoping no one could see
trying to freeze the crestfallen skylight

deep in my eyes
the magic beating so loud
gasping spangles in my heart
dangling there on that tightrope she didn't notice
even though she laid it taut for me to walk high
and I prayed silently as I walked down
her artist's spiral staircase
that I wouldn't drop the tray
glass cups bubbling tadpole galaxies
in your family's place in Neve Tzedek
paused skylight in my eyes
looking up to the ceiling
your mother looking down.

I promised, I'll go to synagogue
if I just make it down this spiral
galaxies and tadpoles in one piece
and your brother chuckled when he noticed
I always liked him
he was genuine
earthy and gracious in ways
your mother was not
and how I wished his Egyptian boyfriend
was there to diffuse your mother
who didn't like my joke about
deboning the fish
I couldn't shake the nerves
I wished they hadn't broken up
why did they have to part
right before I made my way
up and down these spirals
your mother looking down

THE ONES THAT MADE THEIR MARK

so many tightropes
walking spilling
flowers and too much magic
or so I feared
I feared her
as I hid alchemy
its history
like precious flowers
saved in the back of the store
something that felt like a circus all right
magic staining my hands good and wise
I made them invisible that night
as my lost glove
and I couldn't help thinking
about your flickering turns of phrase
an atlas of word alchemy to swear by
roots I thought we both loved?

I would have done anything, really
to moon swing for your poet's heart
that through all those elephants in the room
and tightropes stretched out
I walked
all the friends and family
I circus hoped
I twisted to impress
really I just cared about astonishing you
sometimes I think I let myself love you
because I believe in alchemy
I sure believed in it then
jimmying any bolts locked inside me
after that Sunday we woke up

kindled in bed together
flames stretched nice and high
wordless and wonderfully happy
or so I once believed for a snapshot in time
train rides before.

Your opinion shone bright in our hamlet
well, it was yours
but what was yours felt for a time
like flowers to hold
brought out from the shadows in the back
I felt enraptured by the old city
it was all a tender part of living poetry with you
reading Yehuda Amichai together
you liked living in Jerusalem
a perfect city away from your family, you said
how we'd climb up on the roof of your apartment
just to skim the stars with our fingers and lips
lost in the flowered cosmos
the poetry of taking trains to feel our circus
to kiss you and stamp the world in leaps.

I was blind to seeing so much in the before
what would become our past
how your heart swung higher
tight as a skyscraper rope
growing weary of magic
the stretched faith it takes
to catch such genuine sparks
not meant to be studied
like we do the dust of history
but to be felt beyond ego

THE ONES THAT MADE THEIR MARK

I missed the part where you began
to bubble away like champagne foam
pearls stealing away invisible
before a glove in the night runs fugitive
quiet as an elephant asleep
the country we shared
fish-vanished as if it was a dream deboned.

It still hurts years later
the deeper in this memory I touch
like the heart scars I opened to you
grew their own Jerusalem tree
the rings of love and pain circling
because before disaster hit in Heidelberg
you tried out the word girlfriend
like springtime flowers
singing on your tongue.

You said we were like a boat
ready to leave the dock
the adventure would be one we'd share
navigating answers to questions like
"Are we seaworthy?"
that night I thought we were
so enraptured
in the old and new cities of your touch
mine pressing yours
like petals saved painting pages inside
we missed our Taizu reservation
train-track hungry with blazing youth
adrenaline caught up in our swinging circus
but that was before

disaster hit in Heidelberg
there's a country of time in that *before*.

I didn't see any danger
when you told me
"*I told you you were fire
I personally don't have that energy
not sure many do*"
didn't know that was a warning too
I thought you loved that about me
and it hurts
it *hurts* how you made me question it
in the aftermath of us
because when two poets split
Tel Aviv torn from Jerusalem
a deboned fish leaves eyes bulging
and I could feel the magic shattering
remembering where our bones once were.

A skeleton of love you removed cold
I didn't see how
you could one day drop passion
like I lost my vampire glove
toss me up like acrobatic Northern Lights
to let my colors crash to the circus floor
blazing into a love grave
the elephant in the room staring at me
lighting the way down
with all my contraband wildfire
something brilliant
I dared to show
share with you

THE ONES THAT MADE THEIR MARK

smiling open.

When I danced barefoot in your sunlit studio
because I spotted your poem
"Algebra in the Basement"
on the corner of your desk
with a glance I saw
eyes full of circus hope
that you ended it
"iterating with love"
handwritten in navy
only to tell me
"let's take it a step at a time,
Lady in the Dress"
I was traveling in trains
baring love in my favorite dress
one my mom bought for me
because she loves how I smile in colors
like they've been saved up special
baring stories
like when my father taught me
algebra in the basement
teaching me to solve for "X"
because he loves my curiosity to learn
to navigate questions
all my stories I bared to fuel flickering love
morning dew misty on our hands
I was looking up.

It's only when I take a step
a spiral staircase winding back in time
I can figure out

you had a mind for setting the high wire
all to invite my fire
that burned the tightrope on accident
you stood craving love's rehearsal
a maze you could spend your whole life
figuring out
flints that tumble SOS
history will show constellations
we surfed from Israel rooftops
how they all plunged down
a moment terrible in Germany
passion turning in circus ruins
just the way you loved it most
like the Tower of Babel
it so suddenly translated us apart
fear snuffing out petals from our pages.

Maybe it wasn't
all that sudden
I just never knew
like your mother never knew me
and you both never knew my roommate
who you called boring
I said, a creative genius
not interesting enough, you told me
unless she was sparking smoke rings
and now I'm left to piece together
that she must have never felt safe
to show you all the carousels
twinkling in her mind
and it makes me think
of how you hated music

THE ONES THAT MADE THEIR MARK

if everyone else loved it
a song was ideal
something brilliant
if it could stand The Test of Time
loved only in the *after* of it all
50 years later
and I challenged you then
that there's so much beauty
you may accidentally debone it
if you're letting all that other
stamp your equal and opposite reaction
and is that not pinning your faith
on a stranger's passion
to imagine yours for you?

The tricky thing in reading back *before* is
when falling
the circus feels like seaworthy adventure
I wouldn't have thought to clock the seconds
that one weekend we'd go up in sheet lightning
snuffed out
didn't look in a telescope
to question the kind of splinters
that can't be solved fast as algebra in the basement
it takes boiling
careful
tweezers to be able to remove clean
from a crushed heart
swimming wounded
withstanding what feels lost
questions floating in The Test of Time.

I told you I loved you because I saw it written
I didn't see
you were looking down
cursive words a total three-ring circus
you only thought you meant
that your words could flip like acrobats
leave me revving with brick red shame
all my blazing wildness
my vitality's best flowers
my curiosity aching *exposed*
shocked in time
as if the entire tray of glasses
had gone tumbling
embarrassment crashing
down a sea of spiral stairs
how my nights looked
the ones I navigated after you
I stopped taking trains to see the old city
I would learn to feel the stinging
salt of my flowering tears
tumbling in skylight eyes
like the glow could cry out of me
wishing I could hide the circus mess
so no one could see
for so long I couldn't face what happened
the questions hurt my bones
I wanted to bury my passion flotsam
under your Jerusalem tree.

I was spilling coconut juice
out of my suitcase
the morning I arrived in Heidelberg

THE ONES THAT MADE THEIR MARK

where you studied abroad for six weeks
and I missed you all six of them
aching with the hunger of youth and wanting.

I rode out insanity
served like a revving plate
my maniac boss had been saving up
just to reach that long weekend vacation
boarding my least favorite airline
where their security questions
tend to spiral into
in-your-face interrogations
I thought loving you was worth it all
even though you hadn't said it back
in my mind's mirror I said, well not yet
I really didn't know
I was traveling to see
the end of you and me.

The magic was beating so loud
it was gasping in my heart
and when you told me
you needed to buy ointment
for a terrible butt rash
from using dirty toilets abroad, you said
I foolishly thought that meant
we'd never been so symmetrical
messy and close as cursive letters.

I look back and see the circus of all my naive
thinking it meant something brilliant
deeper than fantasy

rooted passion looking up
it meant something real to me
that you felt safe
so at peace you could show me
your skin eruptions
and I remember Googling
going into the German pharmacy with you
my hand tingling at the marvel of yours
our palms laced with hushed alchemy
even in the misty Heidelberg rain
because the wait of those six weeks
it felt like a long tightrope
when your phone connection was poor
there I stamped my feet in Heidelberg with you
thinking we might hold together like flowers
petals on pages to trace into tomorrow
maybe you'd share all the love
you'd been saving
behind bolts locked inside you
that you wouldn't mind
my awkward duckling moments
like coconut juice fountains
gushing from striped luggage
a clumsy arrival
because as you told me then
"I'm half-duck too."

I remember seeing the Heidelberg castle up close
a marvel flickering even through partial ruins
red sandstone floating on a green hill
300 feet above the city
the sight of the ragged landmark

THE ONES THAT MADE THEIR MARK

twice struck by lightning centuries ago
something that once inspired Mark Twain
a creative genius
but all you saw was murder in the before
like you thought it was cool
pretending a castle wasn't beautiful
denying it
thinking that made you smart
when I know there's magic
searching what can stand
from floating ruins.

Long before Schloss Heidelberg
when you told me about your ex-girlfriends
I didn't think to poke holes in your ruins
after all "history is written by the victors"
you told me that the Israeli girl
the one before me
shared a camping trip with you
maybe she thought she was arriving at a castle
red sandstone love that might have stood
floating on a lush green hilltop
but she couldn't twist into what you needed
you craved an orbit of space
so you snuffed that love out with lightning
plundered the relics to build a house of stories.

I can't forget the vegan girlfriend
who you said pretzeled up wordless
when she stayed with your family
couldn't show you
the grocery list she'd need to refrigerate

so head over heels she tumbled too
your next Gothic masterpiece
I can imagine your mother looking down
and you said it all with
the conviction of a tour guide
showing me ancient history.

I didn't ask enough questions
I saw your beautiful ruins from afar
a tourist to your old loves
hiking the lush green hill
distracted by red sandstone
because when at the circus
the performance asks us to suspend disbelief
if I were to just play our history back
like the record keepers you idolize
notate the pages with crushed petals
I might have seen moments we were
something brilliant
for you to flip in your mind
like the weekend we spent with your family
your mother irate that you pointed out
she called a bag of chips the wrong name
and you sighed on the couch
"Aren't relationships *hard*?"
and I smiled a bit confused
responding, "I don't think they have to be"
not realizing that you want hard
you want challenge
you want murder in place of a castle.

Sometimes I think of

THE ONES THAT MADE THEIR MARK

what future girlfriends you meet
think of me
before you snuff them out too
where my holographic passion fits
in the fridge
next to the vegan's penchant
for lentils or chia seeds
maybe you've placed it on ice cubes
turning us both into scarlet popsicles
you'll thaw out in your retelling
sharing cool answers twisted on a
circus tongue
and by all means
couldn't you have just bought
vegan products for the girl before me
did that have to be such a maze
where her heart must have gotten lost
in the circus ruins that you made it?
Where does my openness
holding an orbit of space for you
like flowers painting passing hands
how I believe in time's calligraphy
trust lacing galaxy hearts
where does that fit
next to the Israeli hiker
who wanted you too much
loved you at the wrong time
and when does the record keeper
start to question if there's an empty circus
in finding fault like ruins
in every tourist's mirror but his own?

You ran in ragged ruins from love to love
hoping to arrive
at a floating doorstep that remains
downstairs
because you and your mother
you don't seem to look upstairs
maybe you'd flip your history
for a manic pixie dream girl
she'd have to be elusive though
deliver a star turn
like a vampire with a missing glove
a vegan to place on a Salem witch trial
or a camper who could oscillate
between needing you and freezing you
in ways that could turn your brain
to champagne fizz
because now I see you wanted to fight
only over the imaginary
so much so you pretended to Van Helsing me
because I was "too agreeable"
when if I translate that
from my side of Babel
I know it's because
I wanted to feel the love between us
see the marvel of a castle
hiding open
standing from the ruins
that Heidelberg night you didn't.

We had spent six weeks apart
the magic was beating so loud
it made your head gasp

THE ONES THAT MADE THEIR MARK

and it must have made you feel
awfully insecure
that I was so understanding
after you challenged me
to *challenge you*
like lightning can rip stone to tatters
knowing what I know now
I shouldn't have swung on that rope
you made my mind excited
and I took your bait
a circus ticket you'd been saving
I wouldn't touch it today
let it paint my hands like something brilliant
I'd see the tracks lead to a fish without bones
eyes running scared
but I thought you were so smart
I wanted to prove to you
I could be challenging
when you were jealous
how I fought with my maniac boss
every day
he got to have that piece of me
"aren't relationships hard?" you asked
conflict was what you craved
a history of it
closing love cold behind your fridge mist
right after heating it up
scatter it boneless into Heidelberg's overcast night.

I've learned our end by heart
rehearsing it over and over in my thoughts
I know I shouldn't have

pushed so damn hard to sleep with you
I can cast my mind mirror like a fisherman
turning back time
reflecting how I ached to show you
I know vividly what I want
in the moment I want it
I'm not shy about that
but that's not what you had in mind
still, I wasn't your mind reader
any more than I'm your lover today
it was a disaster
ever since
while my Kentucky hips
revving with Tel Aviv crackle
galvanized you
you struggled to thrill me
equal and opposite missing in reaction
an awkward moment you didn't find
easy to overlook
as coconut juice spilling from a suitcase.

I have a history of finding grace
I know how to gather it up
a maze of sensitivity
bring it together in a fresh bouquet
holding the stems to share the flowers
but I feel that only made it all worse
like how when stubbing a funny bone
all we want is to rub it
try to distract the bruised nerves
without me playing the mean act
a girlfriend you could say

THE ONES THAT MADE THEIR MARK

made you feel
like the world was over as you knew it
there was nothing to distract you from you
your performance anxiety
stretched taut on a terrible tightrope
it just plain rattled you
revved up what you had kept locked
all that you'd been saving in your heart
the irony is that you set that rusted bar
high as Heidelberg ruins
needing us to moan crescendos in sync
but I learned from you
when you shove
two orgasms like mirrors together
pretending they're refrigerator magnets
of course glass is bound to splinter
love on top of each other someday.

You craved the symmetry
our bodies like conflict lacing up and down
my pleasure could only set sail
rev up
arrive
because you challenged it so
you didn't want any part of my show
if it came after yours
swinging onto your fantasy bars
ripples in champagne bright against skin
you sought to be the orgasm ringmaster
how it unnerved you
to have to try
to light anyone's match

in the aftermath
you wanted to get two flames
out of one match
yours
but that Heidelberg night
we struck disaster
my passion was lost frothy in the maze
like expensive imagination
or a glove gone missing in the dark
all that was left was vulnerability
well, not mine
yours
even then what was yours
it felt like mine
something brilliant
cracking like a train rusting in its tracks
you couldn't shoulder the embarrassment
it spread like a lightning rash
scratching up our sandstone.

I could see something new
flickering before me
a scared boy sitting at the kitchen table
eyes bulging like a fish deboned
this was history you tried to bury
murder I didn't watch out for
looking up at the castle from a distance.

You never told me in your guided tour
before Heidelberg
how loves in your rearview wanted passion
where you came up short

THE ONES THAT MADE THEIR MARK

you grew up running from it
"it's been a point of past contention"
the words echoed
shivering like alchemy coming undone
you couldn't crucify me for it
so I'm sure in your circus history
it sounds good to say
it's because when you wanted pizza
I didn't pick a fight with you
and say *well, I want burgers!*
when really
why can't I want pizza too
why should I play
try to become
your equal and opposite reaction
and what maze are you walking through
if someone loving what you love
loving you
feels hideous?

I can see your face in my history pages
looking down
telling me if you were your father
you'd *run*
when all I could say to you was
it doesn't have to be this way
I took planes and trains that ran to you
and I didn't get it
couldn't figure it out then
the circus I loved was set up
for you to be able to swing away
like a marble moon fleeing the sun

and when you think darkness is genius
you may never figure out
holographic passion
it doesn't have to be
cause for elephants
or you trembling gray in a Heidelberg kitchen.

I've studied in the mirrors of my mind
the time you handed me a card
a dark beetle painting the cover
because you knew I didn't like bugs
playing the contrarian
relishing it
drinking foaming beer outside
your Universität Heidelberg friends
shaking heads
laughing through the foam
they told me how they watched you
swing for the cheaper chocolate
when they splurged on the luxe for their loves
and I could hear my grandmother's voice
stern in my head
telling me, *this boy, he's not generous*
I could hear my father saying,
it's always about more than the chocolate
and I could see my first ex like new
how he played cheap as something classic
I just wanted to curl up to you
not find the symmetry in the Tower of Babel
sitting sideways at the bar in Heidelberg
your friends talking clever with us
my mouth mid-gulp of frothy pilsner

THE ONES THAT MADE THEIR MARK

where all I started thinking by your side was,
oh shit
for the first time
after realizing I thought I loved you.

The night after our first date
my taxi driver warned me
you botched the end of our night
told me the light rail would be open late
but it wasn't
I was looking up at midnight in Jerusalem
and you just stood there
seeing you got it wrong
clumsily offering for me to stay over
but it didn't feel right
staying over only because
you found timing then easy to overlook
so I paid 300 shekels
agreeably
to get back to Tel Aviv.

You acted all tough with the taxi driver
who warned me
wise on the drive back
that he could read *people*
and he said
he could read this guy was wrong
you were wrong for me
he told me full of intuition
and I remember stamping the world
outside my apartment door
wondering if I'd one day come back

to this moment
frozen in the refrigerator bin
something I'd been saving
and sure enough
there between us in a Heidelberg kitchen
cheapened history and wheels deboning time
stamped like a herd of elephants arriving
uncalled for
I couldn't help remembering
that sharp taxi driver
how he could see then what I couldn't yet
how you navigate ordinary disaster
embarrassed
unable to face it
planting the weight of the shekels on me
that's how Heidelberg's disaster felt
like paying 300 shekels
to be told on a long taxi ride home
oh fuck
you weren't who I thought
which cost me dearly.

You started to ghost me
serving up cold Casper
in the weeks after
I had flown back from Heidelberg
and I started to navigate going *crazy*
because I knew this wasn't
how our circus swung
not before
I could feel you running
before your feet stamped the ground

THE ONES THAT MADE THEIR MARK

back in Israel
where the only text message
that seemed to get your attention
was that things weren't going well for me
I told you I was adopting a scorched earth policy
to deal with my maniacal Wall Street boss
and your interest must have flickered
because you like bloody passion
when it's not blinding your vision
as long as it's not too close
as long as it's through
the lens of another's history
you looking down.

At the foot of our ruins
you sat on my bed in Tel Aviv
just landed in Israel
playing pretentious
so generous with it
feet crossed like rusty railroad tracks
a bargain bin Socrates
telling me in word staples that deflated my room
you were ready to break up
because I'm "too agreeable"
which made me laugh
because this was happening because of sex
sex you didn't want to have as much as me
love you didn't want to feel as much as I did
something we actually disagreed about
something that didn't work in your history
you were furious that I initially said "ok"
because after all

this was the next act of the circus
time to make the champagne bubbles fight
time to feel love like a rash between ass cheeks
because maybe that's how you felt love in your home
where magic meant
the end of our world as we knew it
I took your bait as we sat there
love getting snuffed out
tightropes ricocheting off my lavender sheets
your eyes cold and shut as a refrigerator
that you turned into a maze in history.

I was ready to have words with you
peel back the alchemy of it all
take the trains off the rails
argue my case like spitting out snake poison
because I'm my father's daughter
I know how to arch my ruby tongue
a bow and arrow when I have to
I sat on my bed trying to translate my soul
but the thing is
before Heidelberg
I really thought our letters laced in symmetry
and it was only at our end I realized,
oh fuck
this feels all wrong
why does loving you feel so sad?

I sat across from you
hiding how I wanted to shake
in the after
I watched elephants crush

THE ONES THAT MADE THEIR MARK

the alchemy we'd shared
stamping it with gray feet
Kentucky neck hot under the collar
your pseudo-meditative chill and my chagrin
trains wrecking each other
turning my bedroom misty
feeling Heidelberg hurting all over
love spiraling
asymmetrical in that Tel Aviv apartment
I pushed to have you see me
the way I saw me
twisting for it.

All of that
now makes me feel like such a fool
I sometimes wish I could
take a time train back to me and you
bring a cloudless magnifying glass
shake the dust from your words
tell the girl who thought this was
a fucked up circus apocalypse
caused by holographic passion
well, mine
I sometimes wish I knew pages before
love isn't proving
running down spiral staircases
carrying breakable glass
I can feel you sitting across from me
even now wanting to clip galactic flames
like solving an algebraic formula
back then I snapped the stems of my words
looking daggers

"You took a corner of a painting
and called it a painting," I said
getting good and angry
which confused you because you liked that
"I took an impression of a painting," you retorted
I fired back, "It's *your* impression.
It's not the painting."

You left that night
not knowing what you wanted anymore
honestly, you probably never did
like your mother never knew me
and never knew my roommate
though convinced otherwise
you could swear by it
but the two of you look down
and I think that's why
you don't really know the florist
you don't see your vegan ex-girlfriend
she must have felt anxious over oat milk
in a house that on the outside looked beautiful
so many others you've written off in judgment
I'm sure of it now
in the after
you said you needed space
a whole orbit
to think harder
study us some more
and in that time I called my brother
I didn't tell him what caused our crossroads
I only asked for his advice
because even though sometimes

THE ONES THAT MADE THEIR MARK

my brother can be my equal and opposite reaction
without trying
I love and trust him and know
he's smart beyond books
he sees people
a historic gift passed down
that he shares with me
so generous no matter the lessons I face
and he told me my problem then and there
six months in
my boyfriend could picture a life without me
"That's not it, Jules."

I called the friend who feels like a sister
I've known since the age of five
she was floored
almost didn't believe
you could be my passion's challenger
she hadn't felt that ticked off
since the years I loved
my first ex-boyfriend
"Julie, no"
my other lifelong friend Lydia
saw the humor in the circus
told me to write it down
on Tinder and my resume
too passionate
too agreeable
I texted you at 3 a.m.
by the time all the "too" words
had tangled in knotted tightropes in my head
relinquishing the circus of us

the costumes
the playacting
I tore up your beetle card
wanting to float it out the window
but recycling you instead
not wanting those shreds
to stamp the world
that was over as I once knew it
train tracks revving with the promise of more
for all my aching "too"
I texted you goodbye
knowing that I loved Christmas and you hated it
that your history of us was a fraud
that you weren't as smart as you pretended to be
and I got smarter the night I let you go.

Maybe 50 years later
you'll think I stand
The Test of Time
50 years too late
collecting the dust of history
and maybe in half a century
it won't hurt like this
to remember you
castles and murder
the fire you snuffed out in Heidelberg
I'll see without scaling tightropes
that I don't have to gasp my magic in
like a rash you want to erase
that my passion in any translation
through any spirals
isn't ordinary

THE ONES THAT MADE THEIR MARK

standing on frothy champagne pearls
looking up at houses and neighborhoods
and this poetry disentombed
holographic love I carried
in one piece
stamping soles new
wherever I arrive next
I'll just know
train running
somewhere brilliant
tracks of life painting wheels wise
alchemy tickling the roots
finding symmetry
past torn circus tents and tickets
in tomorrow's after
I'll see it clear
looking up from my side of Babel:
How my tender heart was seaworthy
all along.

WHENEVER I DRINK

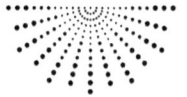

I'm hot-and-bothered
like a revolutionary's gunpowder
at Saratoga
a long ago October:
Old-fashioned faith
click, tick, peal.
Consider me your
ancient aphrodisiac
as you take my desperado bubbles
outlaws straight to your rugged mouth.

Can you keep a secret?
I pop open
heat of July-time smooth
like rich New Orleans
kindling chicory jazz
Café Brûlot Diabolique devilish
mystic from saxes after hours.

THE ONES THAT MADE THEIR MARK

Sing me to champagne froth;
I'll be your favorite fizz bop
I know how to whisper
coffee lips of a brain-teaser
enchanted to brandy chest.

Oh but lover,
I'm so much more
than his last absinthe pick-me-up.
I quench Israeli deserts
mouthing Moulin Rouge poetry;
gulp me like the depths
of a Mediterranean peach
all that's juicy spilling like
Eve's blush and froth
might-and-main
damned with knowledge
in awakening gardens.

So many wisdoms forbidden
and now I learn
tasting them
one by one on you-
Revelations shaking baritone
down your spicy Adam's apple.

TO MY WHISKEY LOVER YEARS AGO

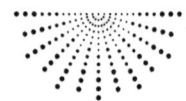

Some whiskeys before
my Dutch courage eyes met yours
my nightcap arms crossed
next to a boy from upstate New York
let's just say
he took me home early
one too many times.

His fingers didn't flutter
breathless on mine
not close enough to give me goosebumps
such paper moon energy
my date sat glued
cardboard-snug
curved to the social table
and I felt like a doll
sewn with button irises
left with the packaging on

that untouched kind of gleam
wanting desperately
for someone to come along
and crinkle my box
someone who wanted
to push pretend out
to touch
to imagine-
A whirl of doll dreams
until I saw you there
and remembered how it feels
to play with my heart awake.

The room seemed to walk with you
wonderful bear arms open
standing there by the bourbon
with a look that seemed to clink *cheers*
leavening light
so real
I realized the revival in my own.

That's the plastic night I forgot
about the date I walked in with
clean-shaven and polite
and I went home
wanting you a rye year later
horseradish days I harvested
moved that life would have us meet
again
a place in time we could find
a quartet of peach tree cheeks
filling out

in the still of unwilted winter
seeing there's so much life
touching misty glasses with you
pouring a shine
lit-up like bourbon
soaking fingertips
amber desire brought back
from months of young hibernation-
Oh my dear whiskey lover,
years ago
for you I parted with the shelf
in a ruby wink.

I wish you knew
that I thought you were
so strong and smooth just standing
there as you were
because you wrote me a letter years later
to tell me you lost weight
you ate salads
your job brought in good money
and I wanted to rinse your glass out
so you could see the crystal kaleidoscope
through my eyes
that the peach weeks we shared
touched marvelous planets in me
a one-way ticket that shepherded us
you and I both
bathed in becoming
that the numbers you shredded
I wasn't casting up to count you out
I wish you knew I felt safe

THE ONES THAT MADE THEIR MARK

heart-wanting
time liquid in your wonderful bear arms.

You weren't meant to be my dearest love
I drink that awareness
with well-aged nostalgia
oak notes like arms unfolded
in my swishing glass
just like I know I wasn't meant to be yours:
You wrote me on Valentine's Day
and this year you were married.

I thought,
I hope that you
the man who took my heart off the shelf
once too afraid
to trace my pink tongue with yours
so deeply you felt the beauty
of our bourbon twenties and thirties
swaying hopeful
for a moment our chance unbuttoned
hands touching the best hummus in town
wandering through whiskey air
adoring those amber beginnings
driving to rose-kissed distilleries
noticing wooden barrels and feeling like
love could age well
like the bottle your father brought out
just for the occasion of meeting me
the finest bourbon I've had
among true company
I hope you found it with her

your blushing bride
on the other splash of the world
the love not meant for us
I hope you found bottles full of peace
beyond measure
sparkling kind
against your hearthside hands.

I hope you know
I'm glad we held onto a *cheers*
in a moment anticipated
unbuttoned seven winters ago-
I wanted you
for exactly who you were
and though I left us
sure you were meant to love someone new
I could still pour the rosy cheeks
peaches from Southern trees
coral heart's desire
we saw in one another
even for a gentle sip of bourbon's time.

THE LIONHEART BURIED IN THE MARSHLANDS

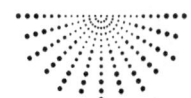

I can hold onto your mechanic hands
so powerfully built
sinewy with instinct
fingerprints on fingerprints
as if I'm just meeting them
all over again today
they could reignite a searching soul's faith
wonderfully intangible
glimmer of rolling strong
a quiet holler engine racing in those eyes
a deep shade of raw earth turning lush
curious with lionheart
electricity mystifying
my favorite American kind of handsome
jaw-dropping rough fingers
I loved that they softened around my hips.

You think I've forgotten

but that's not true-
I remember
they could fix crossed hot wires in cop cars
piece electricity together
spectacular in sparks
but could never untangle
trauma nonsymmetrical
hiding jagged fossils
a secret museum of those you've loved
that most would never know
sweet vulnerability you'd allow to live
for an electric moment
when you'd connect your stranded wires
tangled with the yearning of mine
that have been built
to withstand the heat
even a lurking frozen circuit
a time bomb waiting to rupture
the rapture of a heart's risk.

I feel your wires far
a lionheart healing
somewhere in Louisville
on a Tuesday night like this one
not-so-secretly following my
Instagram snapshots
incredible canyon hands
I sometimes still
pretend I can feel
on the other side of my iPhone
touching when I see your name
flash the memory across my screen

THE ONES THAT MADE THEIR MARK

with once upon a time wanting I subdue
wires I leave free.

I doubt you'd ever know
sometimes I want to send
an olive branch unplugged:
I stopped hating you
such a long time ago
because life's wires run on
perspective unfogged
and even the steam-whispered
wreckage of yesterday
museums I imagine you'll carry with you
can fade something magnificent
in the handsomeness of a looking glass
looking back.

In our heyday
a sunny season long ago,
you would go
by the name of "Everglades"
because you hailed originally
from the swamplands of Florida
and I could feel the warmth
of the sunshine state
spinning revolutions per minute
whenever your juiced lips
brightened on mine.

Back in June of 2015
before I chalked my virgin curls
with rebel-may-care purple,

I would have let you
handcuff me to the bed
sirens within us flying
at just the thought
the spiritual palm of another
on tender bare skin
really seeing us
wanting us
damn near loving us
patient witness
for the mess of exquisite wires
that we were.

I felt like I got to wear
your heart bold and big on my thigh
barely under my brushing skirt
when I got that jolting blue bruise
from your tall bedpost
which stayed with me
almost as long as your heart
could bear to be naked with mine
before you self-sabotaged us
poking at wires
both of us immediately wishing
you hadn't
wishing we could call the cops
on the part of you
that desperately wanted
to love all-out electric
but felt terrified of trusting it
when you knew firsthand
the sharpness of a fossil

THE ONES THAT MADE THEIR MARK

in your muscular hand
how it had singed you before.

I know now
the sensitive mechanic
pushed me away
every last marvelous ray
of summer-set explosion
because to bury a lionheart
deep in the marshlands
an accomplice can't be there
to dare you to love
every last short circuit
rotating a haunted museum inside
as you run from and through time
states away.

The impossible risk
shocked you
edgewise:
That I might see
where X
marks
that tender heart's vital sparks.

WHAT HAPPENS TO LOVE AT FIRST SOUND?

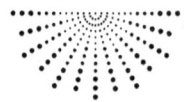

Here's the heart-and-mind
tangle, plain and simple:
I fell for the boy
who sang hushful to the rain,
asking it to step outside
of the unsettled sky,
whose lyrical pulse felt like
an umbrella wound up for me.
That boy lifted droplets
the lightless looped
tuned, turned into musical couplets
clasping watery hands
under the together-shelter of
weeping clouds.
That is the boy
who was the first
to unwrap my love,
soft snowbank opalescent

THE ONES THAT MADE THEIR MARK

before gale-proof boots
trample all over the
milky dazzle, untouched.

I liked the sound of
sharing tender words,
that I adore
'hyperkinetic amalgam,'
how it sparks like pop rocks
blue raspberry crackle
full on my tongue.

We'd layer major chords
when I fell into his way.
He strummed ivory and glossy night,
a piano's steel strings becoming
our wrinkle in young time,
discovering each other
acoustics of long curls like velcro
sticking to five o'clock shadow
that blood-tingling rock and roll
first feelings of calloused guitar-fingers
my youth enamored, crescendo
the richest wooden echoes of pianoforte
at my favorite steal-a-way study
the eureka of maiden love's desire
hymns unfolding
symphonies that could melt Jack Frost's
icicle soul sound-shimmering
dewdrop crystals suddenly romantic
quantum leaps inspired on college grounds.

'It's love at first sound,'
I thought.
Intuition blind;
spot his music signature invisible
to my wonder eyes wide-open.

I had yet to know
how these musician
hands can clench,
knuckled and breakneck.
How could I see that
the lips that glazed and dazed
my naive smile
with southern firecrackle
would shell-shock my mind
with the ugliest refrain?
My first love was violent rhapsody.

When I was six,
I burned my tongue
from drinking hot chocolate
seconds too fast.

He left my heart like
my innocent taste buds-
A bit too charred to feel
anything but singed trust
like staccato sixteenth notes
against the roof of my mouth
for countless choral
bubble sodas
to follow.

THE ONES THAT MADE THEIR MARK

If I met him again today,
I'd eat him alive
sour apple fizzy
crunch,
bending his coffin notes
with my voice
an unfrozen river tunneling
out my throat.
I'd twist those chords
something vicious
before he could
turn on me with
a heartsore key change,
spoiling hurricane-rotten for a fight.

When lovers and melodies start
so candy-sweet,
untasted,
it's thorny to feel
when that song's charm trickles
off.
The pitfalls of a new first:
Sitting duck,
when the banana skin of intimacy
erodes.
After all,
when is that waspish moment
a bop on the radio
flips from earworm fetish
to overplayed track?

The first time we broke up,

I sent him home with
my favorite baker's dozen:
Heartbreak-lite
banana nut muffins.
My heart bled in vanilla extract tears.
Even then, I was gifting him
brown sugar mercy
affection for the taking.
Parting stung sorrow-sweet
as if Shakespeare tried to
flutter away on a pecan swan song
a kept retreat
handed over to be eaten.

Though I tried,
pulling away lacerated
guillotined
the silent space needed to suspend
what it meant loving
him in vibrating strains.
Should I have un-loved him
in slow seagull
punctured balloon breaths?
How could I bundle
back up
from where it poured
yawning
all the serenade and lilt,
the fall, the cadence
after I'd let the dawn of love
spill
revolve

THE ONES THAT MADE THEIR MARK

enmeshed in his yo-yo static?

Even after the Judas kisses
mounted and slighted
and played me false,
I didn't know how, when
to hear the coda;
not even in a gush of cannonade.
I grew deaf to the sonic boom.

This was years after the boozy
could-have-been crash of
his thrumming gray-green Ford Mustang,
had I not fought him for
the teeth-edge of his car keys
I pinned against my
excusing palms.
My mother hated him
without knowing
the half of it.
But it was love at first sound:
I was in gasoline-deep.

I still remember the night
I locked him out, left to cool off
the dynamite I'd explain away
that was his temper;
Thwacking at every
window in the rain.
His piano keys
always obeyed those
calloused guitar hands-

And how it set him off
that I'd ever release
dissonance.

He dared me
when he issued a mock warning:
Who on earth but him
could play me?
He said he accepted me-
If who I am is ballads,
and for this acceptance
I *owed* him fairytale grace
under the fright-frost
of weeping clouds
that once brought us close;
He saw me as crushed damsel
torn rose petals to blush
days in the sun
when the maestro conducted
between snap switch
toggled to sing birdsweet
for his composer fingertips,
pianississimo,
forgive his spook in
fits of minor scale sweeps.

He never found my
overcomer anthem.
I played it louder than
his hyperkinetic rage
hidden
like a trap door

THE ONES THAT MADE THEIR MARK

under the damper pedal,
I learned to lay it over
the lovestruck notes
he swallowed
between cheap burgers
and turkey sandwiches
ordered for me.

I spent years and worlds
switching alternating records
in played out jukebox love
just to prove him wrong.

I turned off his song
four years too late
in my garage,
leaving him clutching a
milkshake he bought for himself
with a rundown coupon,
in tuned out plaid flannel.

I'd later hear he smothered
a bird beneath his
careless drunkard hands
on his empty couch.

Every time I hear
Kentucky cardinals
sing aloud
rosebud anthems
through
storm-grown freedom trees,

I take my bubblegum tongue
to the roof of my mouth.
I don't touch
our family's wooden piano
for years.
I shelter the chords
crackling and wise.
Never to tip over with
half-priced bulldust.
Dazzling milky
as untouched snowdrift
sculpted in lullaby winds.

I let them breathe
in neon measures.

A PEP TALK TO MYSELF IN THE MIRROR

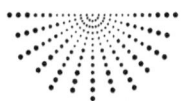

My Casanova has gone missing
and I'm barefoot exasperated
in the bedroom of my Tel Aviv apartment
that feels a little too bankrupt tonight
driven to distraction.

As I toss back honeysuckle Moscato,
my kiss-curls and lovelocks
bounce just above
the small of my back:
I'm feeling out a rich memory,
that once spilled over
Miss Sass-afras lips-
handpainted,
tiled in glazed edge
fireclay.

The 42 year-old Israeli
hedge fund manager
talking Wall Street to me
at the Valentine's party
where the Young Israeli
half his age
brought all the allurer-confidence
in the crowded room
to its knees.

If a force field shifted human,
that's this Young Israeli,
turning me his lit cigarette
like old Hollywood detectives
and starlets in the '40s
as violet lightning as he rattles
Mr. Hedge Fund into
hissing firewood-
A fizz-crackle in the background.

So unfazed,
coolly walking up behind me,
like the curve of smoky moonlight
washing ancient Masada's
rocky fortress,
before peak sunrise butters the plateau.
I feel how his firebolt energy forks
flashes, gallops a hungry amber orange
seconds before I meet his touch
learn his hand that codes
Iron Dome

THE ONES THAT MADE THEIR MARK

defense
against short-range rockets,
master interceptor,
a red-blooded hand that
surrenders just above
the small of my back
I feel it as I hold my empty glass
rapid-fire bubbling
pearly with Gewurtztraminer.

Our glasses clink
and I see spark plugs run up
against each other
such silent fuschia intrigue
laying open
exposed
beautiful seduction
in a crowded room.

"L'Chaim!" the young Israeli says
those damn blue missile eyes
heady with defiance.

He's only young because
he's meteoric
invisible rocket fuel dash
I feel it
in every violet word he speaks.

I tell myself in the mirror tonight,
J-

He's young because
he's a zooming boy
come-hither aerodynamics
without a John Donne compass.

He looks like classic meringue though,
I remember-
So good I can just comet
in all that's glossy
so delicious
eggs in a bowl
separate
without thinking twice about it
any leftover refrigerator chill
adapting to the temperature
of any room where he is.

My mirror snaps me out of it-
I remember that the boy
cracking codes
can't stay glued to
the southern target.
For a while,
it made me question
if my starlet lips lost kilowatts
every time he drank
my radioactivity.
Did they?

But that's streetwise reason-
And I didn't choose
the man at the party

THE ONES THAT MADE THEIR MARK

who bragged about hedge funds
not realizing I can read the stories
that circle the bent numbers
not realizing I've written some
that made those numbers sail
some that guided them
stumbling to a crater.
I can be powerful too.
I'm not impressed by a skeptic's money
that just goes on to fold angular in his pocket
hidden from marvelous breath
how it can swoon higher than numbers
pulses curtsying on mountain tops
that feeling when you meet
someone delicious-
It can't be bought.

I'd rather pay attention to how
I found zero gravity
just holding the stem of
the Young Israeli's bubbled-up glass
even if there came days
he made my breath sail
and some days he lead it
stumbling to a crater
with the same cool nonchalance.

I'd rather cross by heart
how he absorbed me
through the mist in his arms;
carrying me across the beach
in front of a beachside restaurant

a place I loved
because he took me there
lusciously attentive
in some snapshot moments
as if he was
playing for keeps
across the quartz-glinting sand
us in the kicky hush
of flying night.
No one could see
at the rooftop party
on top of the cordless sea
how the Young Israeli
lit lightning rods
under Tel Aviv's Hollywood
a hot shot movie director
in his bedroom
hiding in plain sight
Benjamin Franklin walking in Israel
discovering I could make a corridor
channel electricity
the kind that could pilot
aerial pillow to indented carpet.

How I'd float through any
black holes and stars dancing dizzy
to be a flexi-straw stirring cream
soda in our island universe.
In the eureka beginning,
I was dayspring- the main attraction.

When he strayed

THE ONES THAT MADE THEIR MARK

I can imagine
he chose to direct different scenes
secret.
My heart hissed in a forked crackle
singed in the background
those nights he went missing
so I traded the Gewurtztraminer
balancing rosés and Moscatos instead
between two palms.
I feel now
like my pulse has been tattooed
changed by the delicious
discoveries as if I found out
the world isn't flat
but I'm still somehow left navigating
my soda rocket ship back to earth
captivated by its roundness;
I desperately want to forget
how the glass used to fizz over,
electric never-love
unsure if we'd ever touch lampshades
had Benjamin Franklin decided
not to fly that kite.

Not once did I ask
if the
slowly
disappearing Israeli
got lost somewhere
tripping on youth untethered.

Somewhere

in the fleeting whirl of Tel Aviv,
a Middle Eastern bottle
of New York races
and California Coast swims
what's familiar meets delicious and new:
a foreign fantasy land
cooking up elixir
it kisses five-star;
my tongue like copper
becoming electric gold.

There's just something
about a charged Israeli man
with eyes telling of
electromagnetic whereabouts
sea flashing sky,
hydro yin to my yang
I feel thirsty
dying to reveal
my undercover wildfire
because it's been there hiding
in plain sight
in so many crowded rooms unseen-
Venus flames that know
how to break liquor-engraved ice,
melt it pure north
like they've been on the run
for centuries,
hush hush.

I find orbits for
these men who

THE ONES THAT MADE THEIR MARK

unhook me bold
like my favorite black lace bra
that cost me a few numbers
but was worth its whispered charisma.

*God, how I love
how we mushroom into a smoking gun.*

My mirror glints back wise:
*Let go
we don't need their smoke and haze*
these salacious
blue-eyed spells
Young Israelis cast
the ones I fall for
just to taste
the way lightning kisses kites.
So I let the last electron
fall
tall to the crater,
a bewitched petal
blazing in the tossing sea wind.

No smoke
none of that haze,
this is me
without his body electric:
Star-dancing off
softest springs I've devoured
and wildest winters braved
eras I've hibernated in graves
memorizing the still roots of patience

so I could erupt
a forest of passion
something he drank with blue eyes closed
somehow I bet he'd only see
a garden dress cascading to skin in a mirror
when this is my flaming sea
sparking up maddest corridors
inspiring buried pillows to grow feathers
night flying
crackling high as his heart through my chest
living voices up past rooftops
black lace underneath us like rockets
mushrooming into a smoking galaxy
impossible glitters and stories
I've written with my pink mouth on bubble words
ones that wrapped around numbers
ones that once brought him incredible
to his knees
all that he's missed untethered and cordless
this is me swirling into a fountain geyser
he'll wish was his for the taking.
He'll *wish*.

I enjoy my bare knees swaying
as I come up against a rare bolt
lightning unhooks me bold
in black lace alone
in here I discover
no kites
I just feel it out like wisdom
hot off the press
it kisses my sparkling tongue

THE ONES THAT MADE THEIR MARK

the rush of new beginnings
how they mushroom into
a smoking sea
mirrored back at me
a reckoning delicious
on its own
I hold this seaside copper
flames that inspire sorcerers to kneel
knowing they can't be bought
they can't be stolen.

Any time now
I'll master it
directing centuries on the run
carrying elixirs of familiar bottled new
where someone beautiful might see me
across a crowd
past numbers bent and maddest corridors
impossible glitters and stories
in rich terra-cotta eyes
living electric gold
telling of electromagnetic whereabouts
worth their whispered charisma
but tonight
I see me dancing in my own mirror
feeling out the shape of my soul
it's plenty for my earth roots stirring up
patience like Franklin
tasting eureka.

So much they miss untethered and cordless
when I'm dying to reveal:

It's not just youth that fizzes over;
while kites fly
like night through storms,
I've found some thunder sweeter
than even rooftop Gewurztraminer.

CHAPTER 3

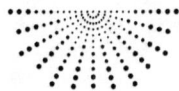

INSIDE THE HIVE OF A COCKROACH

THE DAY I TOOK OFF MY GLASSES

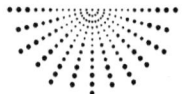

I remember in 4th grade,
I caved.
Back then,
a white flag looked an awful lot
like owl-rimmed glasses
on a small Jewish nose;
too big
for my
narrow
face.

Suddenly, blurry needle-leaves flipped
focus:
Neary silver-blue
evergreen trees
turning crisp
before my saucer eyes.
Moving to and fro

THE ONES THAT MADE THEIR MARK

as if balancing a new
Hello!
in the wind.

I could see.

Once upon a time,
Cocoa-cinnamon frizzles,
chocolate locks growing,
bouncing
over my first fresh pair:
rose-colored glasses.

Close-up
on 9 year-old me
captivated
with white chalk and dreamed-up visions
dancing in unison
on pavement.
If my feet got caught on shoelaces,
I'd fall face-first into
the "Island;"
a happy and tucked away
patch of suburb-green grass,
framing home.

But the day I took off my glasses,
there weren't garden leaves
floating.
No gel pen
suspended on my right ear.
No Barbie-pink shoelaces

curled in almost laughter.

I jumped so high
that I spit out your rusty nail.
And there they slipped
right off my Jewish nose.

Somewhere where
Wall Street
framed
Tel Aviv.

Startled frames
turned tessellation
on
grizzle-gray concrete.

My eyes aren't blurry now-
I can count their old stars
playing hopscotch
between crooked rose rims.

THERE'S NO ROOM SERVICE IN HELL

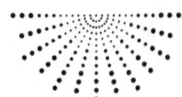

I hope one day
You get upgraded
To your own deluxe room in hell.
Where room service pages
Are lined
With the wicked lies you've told-
The ones where when caught,
You would smile.

I hope the book on your splintered table
Is a How To for Sociopaths-
Written by you.
Your name in black bold.
Let them know the author in hell.

After all, you're an expert spinner
Of spiderwebs thick with
Truths you've bent, c-c-cracked.

Your manipulations dangle
Like a single silver thread
Taunting.
You try to order me-
Because to you
Bright young women are just a la carte.

You're a damned dick-tator.
I'm always one page ahead.
Welcome to my hell for you-
A hell beyond your control.
I hope then it dawns
From that windowless pit-
Where the key turns
And your suite opens
To a den of mud
And thieved joys
Stolen on a warped joke-
Nothing more, *no more*.

AN ODE TO THE COCKROACH BASTARD

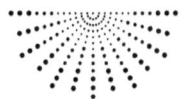

I look at you like a cockroach-
You'll always survive nuclear warfare.
Ugly creatures with shells like you
usually do.

But I've now clocked the man
moth-eaten behind
the belly of the machine
and you better believe
I paid bone-chilled attention.

Here's the scared up
decaying secret
you never wanted
me to smoke out
in all the cobwebbed mind games
and swarming insect power plays.
That's all you'll ever be-

A slimy shell
burning exile in the back-breaking
shekel-shackled hollow
where you buried yourself
imperious
until you see
you lost your longed-for right hand
bloody out from under you.

I hear you linger
stalking those breeding grounds
like an immunocompromised host
crawling in your own exoskeleton
strobe-haunted by the
psychedelic ghost of me
flying, waking up out of your hell-

And here I walk the earth clean
hands to soul untethered
disappearing in my nuclear
submarine fleet
you didn't see coming
you didn't pick out leaving
never looking back.

THE 72 SECRETS YOU PUSHED ON ME

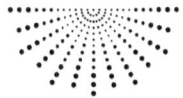

There's an under-the-table
unmentionable
a no-no in business
that the grand old boy's club
tends to let slip with a
"He's being a good boy now!"
firm *mmhmm* handshakes
among men who feel like visionaries
in jeans and company t-shirts
a big money yes
covered in plastic
Polish because you said
the brand is cheaper
just like your hollowed-out
scavenger insect gully heart
burning a perverted keyhole
smoke screaming through my
plaid skirt pocket;

Some ghost doors you opened
sharp-cornered and still wrapped
in your Dr. Jekyll's spook
gear-shifts
when Mr. Hyde would rise
when you let what you called
the 20% worst of you
spin and jolt
hijack the steering wheel
no one to see you
no one to care to stop you.

Four corners, each one of them.
Seventy-two secrets.
Gothic Frankenstein's monsters
if anxiety incisions
and corporate lesions Victors let roam
stilted
if ghost doors and office walls
could speak.

In some ways,
they made you the creature you became
with a private spacious room
three walls and a door
and a sign that said "Sharper" outside
that sewed together your grotesque evils
and gave
the 20% worst of you
filtered air to
squash my breath
as big city days and news spiraled

THE ONES THAT MADE THEIR MARK

inside and on displays,
two screens each- at one point
the envy of the office gossips.
When 20% shocks and gnaws at
the zest and bliss around me
90% essence clipped
at the mercy of
Israeli Wall Street's crowbar
your not-so-secret to the rest
your ghoulish cast of mind
I think of your preferred phrase:
Take those claims of 20%
with *a grain of salt.*
You wanted to tank my stock
but also own its advantages
just for you
and count the gains
rising like Mediterranean tides
that I'd rarely see
an American immigrant
vulnerable
as if you ordered me
rare
a bowl of hopes and comfort tides
you held down like a work wife
requirements I didn't read
in the contract
you trained to impress
and dress down with your strategy eyes
secrets lost in overtime, overtime unpaid
between, behind walls and ghosts
and creature-stoked fears.

Who could bother to pay attention
to the American immigrant's
fading happy?
Who could bother to place
the case of missing Julie joy
"I don't know what happened-
She just *changed*"
dare to point at Professor Plum
behind walls and a door
cornered with the 20% worst of him
secrets and 72 commands
a company leaves unchecked
leaves out of contracts
when Dr. Jekyll and Mr. Hyde
together score high on Google.

I think of the postal box
eBay and four corners, nameless
an accidental state of affairs- yours,
you mailed to my childhood home
and how your laugh twisted its way out
when you said I'm oh so lucky
you even gave me a
floodlit bug-eyed warning,
wagging your index finger
and I hate that I laughed along
like the time my dear friend in college
had a new friend on campus
I so wanted to like me,
to understand me
who tested the waters
and joked

THE ONES THAT MADE THEIR MARK

"How many Jews can fit in an oven?"
and I didn't tell her
that my grandmother
my Neny
younger than we were
as this girl made this pain comedy
tossing her long ponytail back
waiting for my laugh to twist out
my Neny and I of course knew the answer
to grandparents my mom never had
it was that kind of scavenger hollow laugh
like tin can telephone empty
and I knew my part was to play along-
Now I keep it all as proof
under my bed
on the fleecy carpet I've walked
barefoot
on the carpet where I
used to play Spanish tapes
"Si Se Puede!"
my mom sashaying Spanish hips
laughter that didn't twist its way out
it lilted, it cradled,
it taught me what tides-rich is
trust dancing from
pink and blue painted flower wall to
yellow and white-striped
painted flower wall
four walls,
one beaming with six windows,
except now there's a
cheap plastic memorial

for the raise I hear you
gulped
out from under me.

The first week in July
I took on days
I'd make home near the market,
learning to talk Wall Street
as I'd become familiar
with saucy tomatoes
exposing delicious hearsay
from shakshuka skillets
to unguarded mouths,
open
curious craving
main-dish hungry.
I took on years I'd make ends meet
between
balancing on green shoulders
crow's pose
on yoga rooftops
warrior II
Half Lord of the Fishes
I stretched, contorted
up through a bank of cloud
all to say namaste
life in Tel Aviv as your protégé:
I didn't know my job would be
to tame the wolf behind the door.

And I think of the boy
in my brother's Sunday school class

THE ONES THAT MADE THEIR MARK

who slipped his hands down my pants
on a Saturday
and all it felt was cold
in a four-walled room in the synagogue
dim and dark
where no one was there to see it happen
but I can still feel it to be true
and how some boys learn to touch first,
ask questions second
and how girls like me find
tides and words can shrink
and shame and anger both turn me red
I think of how in the company I fled to
like a life raft on the tides and hopes I clung to
two kinds of reds nipping at my heels
a secret run: *mayday!* abandon sinking ship
that I can't tell HR in the next interview
that I have to smile
and say this was my 'family' in Israel
but family doesn't massage my hand
not without asking
how new coworkers wanted to know the joke
ha ha ha over beers
of why I left Wall Street
and for once I couldn't let the laugh twist out
and I couldn't package four corners
and red barbed ghosts they won't understand
stolen raises shot at me through the grapevine
because you thought I'd stay and smile forever
even when you told me 'you're like a broken car-
No matter how hard you push the pedal
you go nowhere'

and how the same week you insisted:
'I just told the CEO what a good job you're doing!'
the display of asking me what's wrong outside
the wrong that you wired like a forgotten bomb
and how I was ushered behind walls
when I spat back in your potato head face
'You asked for a car. I gave you a car.
A car doesn't smile'
words I didn't let shrink
fired right to your hair gel
because you still wanted me to smile
because good girls need to laugh
to play along with your gear shifts
your 20% and 80%
your 'sharper'
and the CEO's 'it's all better-
you see it was all just a
misunderstanding!'
And when it's a misunderstanding
it can be funny!
It can be a big hearty money joke
and how Stanley said, "wow you really CAN write!"
because he shrank my hopes and tides first
read my work second
how you manipulated it to be
when I tried to escape to marketing
to find it's the same stale set of four walls
the same stifling corners
just around the "Sharper" corner:
Your 20% pissed as-all-get-out
to lose your stock
that was supposed to be your golden toy

THE ONES THAT MADE THEIR MARK

your wife
the giddy receptacle for your everything
the machine sports car that revved
overtime in stylish colors
that didn't tell slimy secrets to CEOs
like Ivy did and didn't live to see
words or tides aboard ship
whose unfinished story was held up
like a dead carcass
my welcome gift
my first *should have known* to leave.
No, I was there to laugh and smile
even at your 20%
and my oblivious new coworker
couldn't understand
I mean, how could he?
that it just couldn't be fit into a bowl
for him to test my waters
cynical
mistrusting
how I could be so happy
for fresh new walls
how I just couldn't manage
to twist corners
into a nicely wrapped laugh
how the worst part
is your worst 20%
is the only reason I ran
like a stock rising
like condoms and mean jokes
and choke fears
that never should have been delivered

to my doorstep
like tides shrinking and secrets drowning
and Belgian interns you shouldn't
come close to kissing in cars
and humans that shouldn't
be expected to drive robotically
because skeletons aren't Ferraris
and how I'd never expect my dad's
Lexus to smile if the neighborhood is flooding
and even if not
how some things don't get told
on your Wall Street blog
about how those numbers
and corners
and tight walls
get
broken
down
to
become
car words
and why my incredible new boss
couldn't understand
couldn't fathom
my strangler fears
pedal ghosts of your creature rampages
how I was terrified to take a sick day
because you made me come in
with food poisoning
you said I wrote *better in pain*
and how your secrets added up
to a joke I don't find funny *I don't laugh at all*

when they want to know the answer
as if it's a regular punchline
'Seriously, why did you leave Wall Street?'
Because I'm not a broken car
to taunt
I'm not success to boast to the CEO
as your own in public
and my revving smile isn't yours
to box up
and unwrap
and unravel
like Maya's talent for rejecting you
"I thought she was talented
her first week here
but she turned out not to be"
like Ivy's future
for vexing to tell your secrets
"She spoke to Uzzi
she complained about me
she was disloyal"
her mistake.

The secret is
I have laughed
too many times
at jokes and cars
I've had to
take jaundiced moods with a grain of salt
and the secret is I know
how to smile
unapologetic for knowing joy
that I don't have to prove

isn't an American act
it's real, *it's real* as walls have corners
and new companies
don't ask me
to keep such twisted laughs and secrets
they don't determine my talent
on a sliding scale
of my ability to rev inhuman
to smile at what's unfunny,
to keep my beautiful mouth
beautifully shut
to graciously laugh
like any good girl should
when the silly Israeli boss ships
72 Polish condoms to the American protege
oh it was a happy, funny accident
right?
even Stanley thought so
when he apologized for laughing so hard
"I don't mean to laugh- it's just so bad!"
it's hilarious when the money boy is bad
and says
"Don't forget
to bring back my package"
wolf smile big and hungry
when I go home for vacation.

And here's a twisted
classified secret
the first of the 72
that burns a different kind of
ghost red:

THE ONES THAT MADE THEIR MARK

My beginning week there
my start in your office
my opening days on Wall Street
you slid your black chair with wheels
a little too close to mine
the orange one that bends
you made sure to brush your arm
obedient hairs felt against my skin
making it prickle
confused tides
as a seven hour time difference
like Kentucky to Israel
the first of many times
you'd blur creature-human boundaries
as casually as withdrawing
brass shekels
from an account at Bank Leumi.
You may be a brute narcissist
but I didn't see that written
in your cyclops eyes,
one cider and dark rosewood iris
for Jekyll
one for Hyde that verged on lust
and fury-red
I can swear I've seen them all
I can swear you've flashed them all
at me-
But as if looking at a male Medusa
who spoke Hebrew too fast
when laughing with the men in t-shirts
who once three or four barged in the room
me the only girl

the girl in the orange chair
closing the four-cornered door
for a horrible mock second
to them rib-tickling
killingly funny
to watch peril-white steal red on my face
because so much in money land
turns to fiendish game
even when you whispered wedding vows
into my right ear
and my friend Chava found it odd
and I felt myself laugh
as if watching my mouth
snake a cartoon, *yes it IS odd!*
when on the second screen
the display in my deeper brain
I locked away the disturbing
all its shivering, uncomfortable corners
as if I was a kid all over again
wondering what was right and wrong
when that boy showed me
his hand was so cold.

I could feel my street smarts
igloo-freeze to stone
right there in the heat of Tel Aviv's tides
the NASCAR race of trying to please you
finding the office joke was
you could be pleased once in a lifetime
ha ha ha bets on if I'd make it
when they axed the first two
American immigrants

THE ONES THAT MADE THEIR MARK

vulnerable
right in front of me
one girl crying as she carried her box out
them laughing at rumors of what she did
before she made it to money land
and why
did a four-cornered disposable box
of that poor girl's tears
others laughing, daring in the background
make me want to feel special
if I could be so top-notch to win your favor
when others would bite into your wrath
like how you told me you didn't
speak to Sagiv for a year
a point of temper pride
like how my first weeks your emails
made me cry
but I hid my see-through box of tears
so no one could see
so no one could find the joke
and *still* Jekyll and Hyde put on such an act
when you shared too much
about how you liked to get close to women
to 'remove the shields'
like how you brushed arms too close
and it was only later you'd tell me
about your ex-girlfriend
whose arms you left black and blue
and your mother who hasn't spoken to you
in 10 years
it was only later you'd tell me you read
your sister's diaries

and it turns me brick-red
that all I could make out in the beginning
was your brilliance
brazen,
me a foreigner in a new land
learning to talk Wall Street
English and coffee-Hebrew
rising tides hopes tears vulnerabilities
twisting, contorting to fit in
all my American passion to please
the company that knew better
leaving me with the ghost reds of you
a four cornered room
susceptible and shieldless in Tel Aviv.

You salsa-shook up
to put yourself on
a king post pedestal
czar-like to make me small
and it *worked*
worked like a well-oiled car
to set me up to prove prove prove
vroom higher, *vroom* further
work breaks on a bean bag chair
as long as I made sure to sit
in front of you
cyclops eyes monitoring the work wife
and I broke my people-pleasing mind
to become your favorite car
whip-quick and powerful
too busy looking up at your pedestal
to notice you made a cage of those

THE ONES THAT MADE THEIR MARK

orange chairs and bean bags
me marveling at one watching eye
before the other blinked me up
breathe here and
write your emails for you there
because you're too riled to play nice
today
so I need to filter your madness
write the emails
because you say the data department
is incompetent, unworthy
and you say, just *watch*
as you manipulate Sachiel
out of here
and if you're fighting with Chava
I better not help her department
if I do, you promise to read my emails
and I believe you
I believe you
and no I can't leave on time
never
not unless it's to see Kara
and you have to know
always you *need* to know
and you need to decide
and most times you decide:
Otherwise stay 12 hours
and laugh, 'You're mad at me
because I'm acting as if
I'm your father'
and no you're not my father
not even close

and no I'm not seeing Kara
but I lie so I can go on a date
for my boyfriend to get upset
that I don't fight with him
like I learn to fight with you
because he says I'm *too agreeable*
and any time I'm not,
you turn filthy ruthless creature
you unleash that 20%
and the only person to ask
how I'm doing
is the CEO talking to you
to get the report.

Isn't that awful?
How you'd text me corrections
the deep-breath minute
I'd finally leave
for late lunch-
because you couldn't stand
any of my time
in any time zone
not being owned by either
Jekyll or Hyde?
How your jealousy rose
in tides
when I had a boyfriend
and I had to barter
a game of laughs over
playing pool
at the nearby bar with you
to be able to take

THE ONES THAT MADE THEIR MARK

a vacation day
to visit him
in Heidelberg
for the weekend.
One time you answered his call
when I left my desk
to use the bathroom
and to this day
I don't know what was said
just that it brought out
the 20% worst
in you both.

How many times did I laugh
when boys I'd date
would hear about
the big money joke show
the wolf behind the door
and say, 'wow
ha ha ha that sounds illegal!'

So many times the
20% most naive in me
the one that felt your arm brush
against mine that first week
black chair to orange chair
four corners and vulnerabilities distorted
would defend the 20% worst of you
would feel the company chose me
to bite the wrath
so the others wouldn't feel the chill
of your yelping and yowling

ha ha ha Julie has to deal with *that*.
I wonder how hilarious they'd find it
that you wanted to select
your interns
by Facebook stalking how hot they were.

You relished untouchable worlds of power
between clickedy-clack keys.
When I finally was asked
my opinion
years in the making
by newbie self-proclaimed big shot Stanley
who made a big Wall Street show of coming in
to make the company's ship quarters better
and really stayed as long as he could
inflate his own big money ego
I laid out two clickedy-clack letters: HR.
I used to joke all this Jewish girl
wants for Christmas
is HR, *ha ha ha*.
The office gossip is HR,
I was told,
the same office gossip
who I saw was the reason
one of my American friends
got axed
because she complained
to the office gossip
that she was frustrated
she was asked to work when sick.
So many firings became a joke
and that's why I

THE ONES THAT MADE THEIR MARK

the sole American girl left standing
I held tight to survival
feeling that the ship was unsteady
even if that meant learning to laugh
extra gut-cringing hard
at the haunted house way
you'd switch hats
from boss to controlling husband.

I laughed *so* hard
I sometimes forgot
where the lines of the fake joke
washed off into the outside sands.
Just like that boy's hand
in synagogue
was so cold
I could feel the warmth
of my vulnerable
untouched skin
absorb ice from fingers:
My job for as long as I can
remember
has been to learn to melt ice
swallow frost
and make it look easy.
But it's not easy
it's cold
trying to laugh
trying to melt
with shivering heat.

I think of how Adam says to send

a bag of glitter dicks
in the mail
how my brother says
to leave one of those condoms
right on your desk
a gift from your smiling Benedict Arnold
that says to tell you to go fuck yourself,
as I leave
to go to a company
with Santa's ultimate adult gift
to Jewish women who learn to laugh,
HR
that has sexual harassment warning posters
in every bathroom corner.
And I wonder if you'd even
be able to laugh
from Jekyll to Hyde irises raging
as if your right hand
moved without your permission
tides weeping
because no box you ever learned to keep
could tell raw emotions
to wolf-*heel*
and I wonder how you sleep at night
now that you lost the laughter
you took for granted
you took advantage of for miles and miles
because boys don't traditionally learn to laugh
not in the United States, not in Israel
boys like you stomp and touch and rage
and what do boys like you begin to do
when girls like me leave you

THE ONES THAT MADE THEIR MARK

your 72 secrets
your shieldless corners
your hot and your cold
your ghosts red
and your haunted house hats
without someone to switch upon
your sports car manifesto
wrath-bit apart with skeleton molars
tin can empty *ha ha ha*'s
bouncing hollow from corner to
abandoned pedestal
far far behind?

ACID REFLUX ON YOM KIPPUR

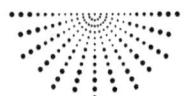

I won't write another word about him-
The cockroach is dead
by the time you read this.

At least to me, he is.
I left behind the sound of a sensational
crunch.

I wiped my feet and didn't catch
the squint of his Gregor eyes
spinning backward
when I sailed around
Wall Street's most dangerous
creepy-crawly iceberg.
As it turns out,
he was only ever made of rubber anyway.
But as Yom Kippur vibrates
solemn rumination around the corner,

THE ONES THAT MADE THEIR MARK

I realize the apology that quivers like
acid reflux in my esophagus.

The future innocent girl
naive, professional
at the edge of her seat
eager to test her fresh mermaid tail
feel how it flaps in a new world
how it might emblazon the waters.

I tried. How I shook the hive's ground.
Bug numbers quaked
under my leaving feet.
The heist of this human heart
was never enough
to save the 'you'
who follows me
splashing
untaught
surely blind to the plague ahead
the ways what's going around
can infect you identity, anatomy, and will
can try to sink your morse code wonder
inner woman tapping through the wire.

I wish it was.
Because now I feel unshackled
flesh and bones in a breathing space
I had forgotten how natural it feels
to let the pieces of me
become my own kaleidoscope compass
hair blowing gentle thunder

thick as thieves with my favorite sea breeze
mad with autonomy's boom.

I hid for you the only gift
I felt I could
that day I headed human for the hills:
An eagle eye warning sign
at the lookout tower
I was lied to
and told it wasn't there for me.
It's there for the 'you'
who follows me
even though I don't know
your name
you must try to keep it
because in Kafka's nightmare
empty skeletons go wandering
go grabbing names.
It's there blinking for those
so-called captains
who make nice and look away
who will tell you you matter
and show you to them you don't
the law of numbers governs
those who willfully don't pay
in needed attention
the law of the hots rules over bugs
and not much else
than a secret gossip chain
charging him with total power
and secretly guarding his antenna
with the weight of it all.

THE ONES THAT MADE THEIR MARK

It still wasn't enough.

To the 'you' I won't meet
and I confess I don't really want to
I wish I could send you my life raft
from an anonymous past naive girl
who once splashed where your tail
will swish unknowing
terribly close to the life-thirsty.

I know I could only ever save the 'me'
who finally got out.
Salvation tolls true as a once fool's gold
the end of the storm coughs
what an exhale
as the voice within
the one I almost forgot
we both make a getaway
with that box buckled
those pent-up secrets
muttering high goodbye
roach Napoleons squirming on the street.
But the broken truth remains, floating-
You'll never know the sorry I feel
I couldn't save you too.

NOT YOUR JULIA ROBERTS

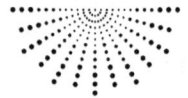

Message in a bottle:
To the Israeli handyman
with fingernail fangs.

You thought you could buy me
as soon as you saw my siren
red lipstick.
You must have imagined
jiggling me wide open,
like a flimsy door
partitioning cubbyholes.
All in a day's work.

I can feel my cheeks va-voom
provoking a prism of reds,
the blusher tinge of your shameless
words careless going bang above
my frozen smile,

THE ONES THAT MADE THEIR MARK

Southern alarms blaring
up to my can't-believe-you eyelashes.
You caught me off guard.

I thought this office would be different.

Hunter, stranger at work-
You should know
my crimson tube is no half-off voucher
for booking a 'room.'

These guava lips kiss coffee mugs
a thousand times over;
Like the sentimental canary pink one
with three white swans floating-
A memento
precious as
anything from my grandmother,
our family's fierce European grand dame.
She wore carnation and fuschia
lipstick she'd cherish
finery frosted upon her
legacy smile.

I'll bet you didn't know that.

You're not the first
to think I was for sale; just because
you craved me.

I'm the little girl in pigtail braids
who giggled

to see my grandmother's flair
pop up on lace napkins
during Ecuador parties;
She threw colors around
in baked triple-chocolate wonders,
on sassy lips
honor-bound
proud
to be a survivor alive.

I'm the teen in braces
daydreaming of her ladylike
paints that could mark crystal
cheeks Kentucky-glow
to watch her become
a U.S. citizen,
speaking Czech,
Slovak, Spanish,
and four other tongues
magnets between her lips.

I'm the wanderluster today
who splurges on
the rose petal trench coat,
who bakes the cheesecake
rich with chocolate kahlua,
who narrates red immortal
on this legacy smile.

But I'm *not* your Julia Roberts.
If I were,
you could never afford me.

FIRST BLOOMS AFTER WINTER

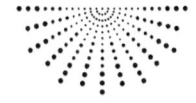

These days, I rustle
under breezy blue mermaid skies
opaline tail to lift
the nod of the ocean
like a sundrenched yes
splashing generous
a wave of algae hums
to thaw icebergs
that seem to mirror
winter's undercurrents
sent to stop and start
bonsai pruning
in the underwater cave
my heart holds onto
like a time capsule
of Mediterranean winter's frost
eaten up;
singsong as a pirate yo ho ho's

who creaky wheel-steers
the ancient ship
sailing big as
peanut butter pancakes
swelling up
against the heat of the pan
as if the stove's sweetness
tastes millions better with
the second and third flips
a pirate who outsailed
a hive of cockroaches
who tried to take the ship
and rob the hull
in cursed cold blood ink
the name of another
they wanted to see
a pirate's tiptoes
make the plank wobble
but this pirate's ship
has sailed pancake-flipping
delicious days
and has hibernated
in tottery frost
and this naval architect
built the pirate's ship
ancient as fairytale guardians
find ways to tap eager dreams
like salt from a cylinder shaker
and a cockroach can name
its salivary glands
can write out *seagull*
or *Poet's jasmine*

THE ONES THAT MADE THEIR MARK

but a thorax with a wrong name
won't ever lift the nod of an ocean
won't smell like repotted tropics
and when I walked the plank
I took fairytale guardians ancient
and a ship cracking frost with me
and I rustle free like wildflowers
on lush green hillsides
in Lakhish,
a biblical city
ancient lowlands
lifting a pirate poet's hello
to mountains that don't pretend
they don't have to
spectacular in the Judean hills
mermaid sky promises whispered
like strong ships in the air.

I take the glistening
dewy doe eyes of spring
above my ancient nose
the nose I've always known
was Jewish-
Spring's eyes are mine now,
and I see Poet's jasmine
on deck
let its sweet vulnerability
lay bare like pancake sails
flipping peanut butter
sticky
frost's mirror biblical
slipping spectacular

JULIE LAMB

from pirate's hands
on a creaky wheel
unfenced euphoria
dewy eyes transfixed
on mermaid skies
guiding the breeze
how to swim warm after winter.

CHAPTER 4

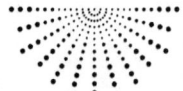

THE HOPE IN PURPLE DARKNESS

FEAR CAN SHINE LIKE PEARLS

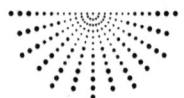

Sometimes I thank fear
just like anger, it teaches
when I dare ask why

BEFORE WINGS RISE

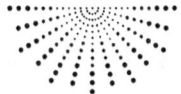

(FOR LEE PENNINGTON)

The wrinkle opens to new
dazzling heights
so that we may feel the moonlight
bright under our wings
the stardust like fizzy clouds whispering
secrets of the universe above
as we survey the magic of all that rises
beneath phoenix feathers
lava swaying in a great triumphant
leap;
this is what it's like to climb into time:
to see the skies we've dreamed of
when we were once as quiet
and low
as the river stones that sleep
steady in a quiet hush
thinking water thoughts

stardust reaching magic down
to the mirror tops that swim
before wings emerge
before wings rise by treasure of night.

SINGING BLUE GATORADE

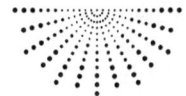

The summer before my senior year
I volunteered for the Speed Art Museum
where an exhibit I loved
was draped in Sam Gilliam's whimsy
mystical fields of quivering hues
lighting up canvas
something that's captivated me
to this day
because
the man said he painted the way he saw
how jazz *sounded*
and I thought that was a well of magic
something that beckoned the senses
to see how music could grow colors
so many moons and knowings before
I took my first trip to Ketamine Land
where I could make out a different galaxy

music detonating in fields of color
amethysts ablaze
not of this earth but the next one
and I remembered Sam Gilliam
thinking, this is how my favorite artists
how their chords
the jumping fabric of hearts
how the plucking of guitar strings looks
and when I get sick
it feels like I'm singing icy tunes
three-part harmony of Blue Gatorade
because in Ketamine Land
there's a poetry to the guts of me flying
though my brain erases it
because in a dimension where
Gatorade sings
the cosmic notes paint
a cappella rhymes swirl
alien hues in yodeling triple axles mid-air.

I discover that even my limbs
fluctuating temperatures
Venus to Neptune
fingers toes icicles all holly jolly
there's a brilliance to the
solar system madness orbiting in me
there's a thermometer tussle to
the nerve of staging a comeback
it takes notes unseen and seasons felt
it takes desperation waded and forgetting
and remembering all that's intense

THE ONES THAT MADE THEIR MARK

dug up in mind fields of vision
revolutions meant to be sewn in silence
remembering to forget too
sometimes takes its own kind of glasses
to climb our way out
strum up
hum hymns on
look over
look ahead
it takes classical and country in splatters
it takes four horsemen I see
who pour water in buckets
a year later
if the dragon slinks
tries to rise up the castle walls in scales
and each time I sing blue Gatorade
and see jazz the way I imagine
Sam Gilliam did
I dip all fingers and toes into
the icy ragtime wonder
of clasping to my heart of the ocean
with all my digits
as I remember and forget
and remember all over again
the depths of my solar system soul
when my guts fly out of Ketamine Land
where jazz and reality harmonize sour
it's ok
because I can illuminate what's sweet
in a loop of sugar cubes
where I learn that seeing this music

means I'm reading frost
melting the kiss of dragons and tails
with the caverns of sheer will and passion
that some doctors forget to factor
and the best ones remember to mark it all
and it's only the desperate wise ones
I think
like Sam Gilliam and me
who know that it takes interstellar fighting
vivid thirsting
clawing like our dragon foes to live
to get drunk on the daylight streaming
of glimpsing such jazzy saturation.

It's then I understand
that when the tape shrieks in a peel
off the inside of my elbow
when the IV is done casting its glow
aliens mesmerized
when all the sticky comes undone
cotton to audacious pulse
chest and rib cage
beating love drums to tinted machines
that it takes swallowed courage
that makes a person
teal in the face
the open and shut eyes of a soul castle
to see how music fills an office
like the room they call 'Julie's'
my lucky jazz stage
where I sing Gatorade and forget

THE ONES THAT MADE THEIR MARK

and remember a year later
this is how I breathe dreams in 3D
the ones only I can see
the cold ones that smolder
and frame what's brave in me
and while no one will ever hear
the metamorphosis of composing
I'm thrilled to wave a conductor's wand
to feel the kaleidoscope of difference
a whole year can make
that maybe the aliens will sway along
and say,
that's how a girl who hopes
looks and *sounds*
in marvelous madness
look at her jazz hit the roof
blow through museum windows
in Roman candles and time bombs
those bright burglars of music sights
it's something to shout about
from eye-opener moons
painting glitter songs
splendor they'll see dripping courage
how I can hold it all
torn and whole in two hands
a brave year of universe keys
standing on melody tiptoes
cupped to this astronomical healer heart
ticking jingle comets
this to next earth
and I'll croon back,

just look at how I sing a year full
the things I dared to come true
improvised from blues
bathing in syncopated beats
draped in the impossible
belting whimsy and ketamine dreams.

MY FATHER TAUGHT ME TO KICK ASS AND TAKE NAMES

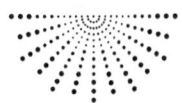

Lips
the color of the inside
of a queen conch
like two pursed shells,
brows wound up
unswervingly brown
and readable as a
snappy grandfather clock.
Believe me,
the jubilant girl
can get
absolutely vexed.

This is my face when
I'm relegated to
'too' anything.

Call me 'too happy'-

'too optimistic.'
Have you ever asked yourself
why is that
such a
gut-wrenching
trespass?
Have you had the
childhood effervescence
flattened out
in you
like a three day-old balloon
someone acid and olive-like
decided for you
was overstaying
its trombone and trumpet
space
play afloat all on its own
in the ballroom
popped
'for its own good?'
Is that why my balloon happy
a root beer float harp
that has nothing
to do with your ballroom
and someone else's bitter pops
to the floor-swept tiles-
Is that why it
seems to almost
offend you?

Dismiss me
if this is how you chomp on

THE ONES THAT MADE THEIR MARK

what fool's bold tastes like.
I don't have the luxury
of winning in a hand
of poker faces-
not when I have my mother's
open-heart hand
scribbled in iambic pentameter
eyes to my lips to
my rootbeer float harp sleeves
all of which seems
to challenge you.
Just know
ruins
long before you smirked
at my happy
have
crumbled
under my withering
stare.
Just know I've floated
over ruins and ballrooms alike.
And I'm not afraid to tell you that.
The air all dances the same
no matter how many days old
the trombones and trumpets sing
like opera frogs.

I fear it would never hover
in your flattened balloon land
that these flamingo legs have
climbed
desert mountains

even when my family
sat in a tight circle
cries of intervention
begging me not to
I climbed Masada
thousands of gutsy feet
above the Dead Sea
at the float of Jaffa-orange dawn
and it showed me what flamingo legs
and trombone and trumpet-eating smiles
what life can do when it's unmistakably alive
in me
I know
I know because these legs have had to float
one courage foot dancing with the air
ballroom vanished overnight
in a suffocating velcro brace
with a spinner
that twisted like a timepiece
the kind old black-and-white villains
might lay out on glued train tracks
their happy lost
popped somewhere under
the sardonic twist of mustaches.
These same legs
that kicked away
crutches flashing
in artificial fluorescent light
as they made an Olympic tumble
to strange tiles so different from
home
my first day at the Cleveland Clinic

where I met Zain
a brave little boy
who you wouldn't know
not at first sight
had epilepsy
freckled and walking on joy
in his Spiderman hero shoes-
No, you don't realize
that these legs that
balloon-step
before you,
trip the light fantastic
are holding themselves
steady as helium
ribbon string doing the samba
to this room's ballroom ceiling
fresh swig of gratitude air.

You don't understand
Spiderman shoes skipping
not when
I had to train my right leg
to walk all over again
after seven months on crutches
planted like a stubborn weed
to the pink loveseat in the den
wondering if I'd ever graduate college
when I spent so many years before
thinking school was all that mattered
without knowing that learning and school
they're not always the same
not knowing I'd one day

kiss an honors medal to
the back of my neck
Louisville sunshine pumping air
into my hot-air balloon grin
no one at the auditorium the wiser.

All you see is 'too happy.'
But you don't know
the ballsiness
the hidden dragon audacity
it takes to hold the coiled ribbon
to float stratospheres above
nerve-confused feet
flame gates open in arms
alligator biting to hands
because chronic pain
called many names
since it first popped up
during the Civil War
Reflex Sympathetic Dystrophy
RSD
Complex Regional Pain Syndrome
CRPS
the ways we nickname
a sympathetic nervous system
whose pain won't stop dancing
all over the place
names I remember
when the burn of the hot compress
doesn't stop on my knee
even after my mom rushes to remove it
Causalgia my favorite doctor says

THE ONES THAT MADE THEIR MARK

Dr. Olson
with his old-school black suitcase
and questions none of the others
who studied in books
thought to ask
so they never found out
his helium answers
trumpets and trombones and frogs
he calls it 'soul-changing pain'
and it can outsmart
when we think it's not looking
and jump right foot
that rehabilitated itself
even after it learned to run the gauntlet
thought it was safe
buried in a small basin of rice
trying to pick up legos
the colors of crayons
boy can it jump
and hop
like wildfire rabbits ranting
and take a forest of limbs
down with it.
But you roll your eyes
outcries of 'too happy'
like you're staging
a Masada intervention.

You don't realize
the nerve of me
to inflate my own helium
and remember Zain

and his skipping Spiderman shoes
I think I'll remember for always
and choose to float
up
up
up.

Yes, I am so happy
I learned to live alive
that my legs kicked away crutches
that my balloon brain resisted depression
like American ruffians
once declared democracy
in spite of King George's
furious how-dare-theys
the great revolt.
I learned to live abroad
and travel bluegrass to Mediterranean
solo
at one time pure fantasy
unimaginable
no crutches to hoist my scared heart
beating sacred happy to my mouth
and so I sunk my smiling incisors
deep into Italian street sandwiches
palmed fresh from the stand
of a family in Venice who were happy
to be cooking a feeling of
sun-dried tomato happy
I tried on a fancy white trench coat
I couldn't afford in Milan
but it was worth it

THE ONES THAT MADE THEIR MARK

to remind me I was
jubilantly
elaborately
root beer float harp-cascading alive.
That when I'm 'too happy'
it means my balloon brain
is flying treason
my heart
that can't play poker
writes truths of living
all over my wonder-struck face
it's
helium-united and rebellious
for which it stands.

So you see me dimple
as I toss back fresh Israeli fruit
with a reckoning.
The pomegranate juice
stains my fingers-
I prefer it that way,
emblazoned,
peeking through my nails-
spilling tales of
conquered worlds.
I'm Hernando Cortés
and I'm one happy conquistador
surveying the Aztec empire
I built
to checkmate.

These are my

stomping grounds-
and I dance flamingo legs
dragons out of hiding
playing
root beer float harp
pride with Aztec icing
lathering sacred happy lips
turned up,
holding onto balloons
brain and heart unpoppable
a great revolt of trombones
trumpets
and fire without reservation;
without one
second
of
hesitation
just like the day
I set aside my crutches
when Cleveland Clinic
taught me to call my happy
Cortés
and my father tells me to kick ass
to take names
and I take no prisoners
even if you're looking at me
cross-eyed
as I wave my Betsy Ross flag.

I am
American ruffian-delighted
on my ninth balloon

THE ONES THAT MADE THEIR MARK

cloud of merrygoland
asking helium questions
searching searching
for juice-stained answers
shinier than a waxed ballroom
gloss-like-new to resist the dirt
the stubborn scratches
the scuffs of life
so lovely that
you missed the mop I used
to treat the floor so nice-
You're taking one look
at two lips
thick with
a sun-dried tomato smile
reading them wrong
when I want you
to put down the poker cards;
Oh if you could just *listen*.

Hear all that triumph
roar
soul-changing
over
the high seas.

LEARNING TO SAVE A FROG

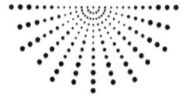

One of the things
that survived the Holocaust
was my Neny's European manners
learning to sit still in a chair
over perfectly angled
shiny utensils
treading sunlight
through the open window
wherever the house is
ours or by invitation
whether served hot empanadas
or scorching animosity
set neatly
on
the special threaded tablecloth.
And that's exactly
what I first learned to do
too.

THE ONES THAT MADE THEIR MARK

Dr. Frankel first teaches me
that my life is a house
one where it's felt uncomfortable
when some guests walk
right by
the sunlight blowing warmth
only to gape
and leave without so much
as a word
and if I'm serving hot empanadas
it's ok to make some
just for my
buenos días hands
indulging.

She tells me it's ok
it's ok
to turn carpenter
to throw together a new fence
to rewire the doorbell to
lift up a yodel
like hot empanadas
when they say they're ready
to fill you with sweet cheese
that guests can master the art
of knocking first
before waltzing in the door
just like I learned to say
si por favor
the ways I learned to give
and give
and give so much

the house felt like a crowded inn.

She tells me that frogs boil alive
in a sweaty pot of
hot kitchen tides of water
simply because
the water doesn't feel like
it's scalding
no not at first
the frog's skin adapts
to the temperature
until it's too late
that damn pot is on a warpath
and the frog alive
starts to die
in *ribbit ribbits*
in an invitation gone ballistic.

And so here I sit
peacefully still in a chair
over perfectly angled
utensils perspiring with sun
door closed but unlocked
bolted for only a few
hot pot kind of people
on sneaky warpaths
frogs letting out
their vintage *ribbit ribbits*
buenos días hands
making hot empanadas pretty
only by invitation
through the swinging fence.

THE ONES THAT MADE THEIR MARK

Dishes no longer empty
from too much giving
at last I can hear it:
I'm only just beginning
to feel the sounds of my belly
full and fluttering duets
how the sweet cheese
I made special
lilts cozy
a warm
indulgent simmer
within.

There beside me
sits a dapper frog
you might spy her from a distance
treading sunlight
lace napkins popping bright
on hot getaway green
trilling lullabies
in rescued ribbits
serving up *it's-not-too-late*
by the pitcher
one of the things
that survived
life's Himalayan stirs:
The pride of well-seasoned liberty.

IT'S A PARTY

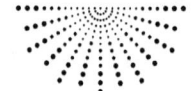

Cocktails in COVID
pearls dreamed up for all our lives
I'll watch through snapshots

PART I

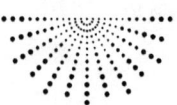

THE SPIDERWEB ALLY

(FOR LP)

It felt like overnight
my sailboat thoughts
searching bygone
smoky quartz sands and metamorphic seas
Southern bones like fireflies twisting
riding rocketship bulbs of light
that marigold color popping
a rhyme of ballet
comfort wings
drama's heart-stopping glow
like a kite with a moving anchor
young at heart
walking away to heavens
with holly tree branches
floating imagination we can see
rose water glossing up the dark-
And there was a secret virus
sneaking up on us all

THE ONES THAT MADE THEIR MARK

no matter where we toed our bygones
that marigold magnitude unleashed
sledding spring winds
from Wuhan to Tel Aviv to Louisville
Milan to New York
from the unspoken promise
of new decade glory
to that feeling of living out
cracked
history
heirloom china tea set splattered
on the floor of our shocked souls
days and nights bundled at once
like the airborne face of time
saved vaporous in knotted yarn
needle sticking through
trying to hold the weaving colors:
And so the dolphin-hipped
owl-howling
world as we knew it
the flower people as we breathed them
went into masks and Lysol hiding,
separating the Land Before Quarantine
caught in drama's heart-stopping dim.

When the sacred bush sat burning,
Moses gathered holy sung secrets
and must have bent his elbows
to hold leather hands to
heaven-lit face
that feeling of living out
floating imagination made real

felt with the force of then and now.

When spiders sew stretch lace,
they bend our minds
as they stitch silver nebulas
showing us floating imagination
comes in all geometric shapes
and sticky thread sizes:
The force of us all
felt in cobwebbed corners
chiffon glory caught swinging in the dark.

When Lee sees the world,
the one we knew,
the one Appalachia grew
from the stone-whispered dirt ground up,
the one between
where the stars thread owl light
and where flower people wake
the unfolding of beginning
where the close of night
opens like a zipper
to the red of earliest bright,
he knows how to hear the
whimsy in the dance
in the soulbeats and dream steps
cosmic strange and delightful
under runaway black holes
drawing in matter
knows how to listen in
to the earth-shake of
deep water rippling light

THE ONES THAT MADE THEIR MARK

on the fins of a discus fish
shimmying through the Amazon
knows how mermaid hearts
tested out inky curses
how sailors swear on smokefall watches:
He understands divine truths
bide their spider time
outstretched
rataplan like almighty acorns
skate universe sighs
down wood-framed mysteries
treetops chewing on bubblegum
right from the edges of sunset.

Here stood a poet
who let his pen glow
humming heart-stopping truths,
like how the dew of sun winds
can twirl sidewise to night
mirror river hands reaching
the dangle of a cloud marble
waterdrops on a lark's beak
before feathers sing out
fluttering with joy
that knows no end to skies
to the love of time's holy burn;
Even when its chin points,
even when what's steady shivers
the force of fairy dust
floating what's real
and what's imagined
in two great infinity arms

sainted forever
by no means
and then
all of us
somewhere brambled
midmost.

I witnessed Lee's allegiance
to immortal web motion
how he trusts moon's devilish
Cheshire smile
mixing up madness
teaching there's rhythm
in coming undone
as much as he hero-worships
the saxophone stillness,
the grasshopper honey-butter notes
that travel rock-kneed mountains
and taffeta hair
long as optimism
drifting in and out
through Milky Way breezes.

So there in towns of
fearless bandaged out-of-sight
in Rip Van Winkle's 2020,
when it felt like
the force of the world
put touch to sleep
so much imagined and real
taking forty winks
and I was left an insomniac

THE ONES THAT MADE THEIR MARK

I didn't see
but I heard the music-words
of this spiderweb ally
who had picked the lock
to cracks in histories
lived before us
who was far from asleep
who was teaching me
there are clear-eyed miles to see
tucked behind those cobwebby holes
where spider kings choreograph
the grace of time's frost eyebrows
raised.

His lessons rolled in
out through the tissued tangle
absorbing bubblegum
reawakening
marigold fireflies popping
in the craze of question mark
days running upside down
of semicolons and commas
and underlines
this piping alphabet soup
that first struck like unpunctual snow
riling up March and April
the nerve of it
at sixes and sevens
with me
a butterfly kite hoping to
sky out
just to lose an anchor once more

and somehow
flying to lose to fly horizon-higher
gets porcupine-pricklier
and somehow
night lighter
crack-of-dawn lighter
each rock-kneed set of sixes and sevens
with my world
a view teetering on anesthesia
with this world's mosaic worlds
pointing a Himalayan arrow finger
time's belly churning
everyone asking "how do we?"
choking on x's, the y's, the z's
before map-reading
with a spoon, milky and unpolished.
Lee's music-words chimed
floating
imagined and real
through the mess of the world
of caterpillar worlds
through those prickly drummer cracks
like a spider's rhyme of ballet
arabesques
as life's alphabet
tried to plié.

PART II

THIS IS THE LAND OF QUARANTINE:

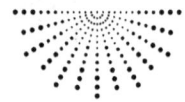

sandwiched next to
boarded-up stores
the fright of flower people's
breath accidentally
catching mine in a hot zone
the loneliness of
dawdling daisy heads
my new nearby friends
when the internet's tremor
delicate as spiderweb
connecting us
determines if my lifelong best friend
can make out my facial expressions
to feel at a jigsaw distance
my tears like cloud marbles
summoning everything-changes emotions
from five-years-old to now
to behold her

THE ONES THAT MADE THEIR MARK

the sheer awesome force
of gorgeous
all that we'd ever imagined
wistfully real
now in a wedding dress store
a mask covering pink cheeks
I've seen grow up
the rhythm of madness
when she feels computer screen-far
and I think of poetry
where it feels letters
they get to wear tuxedos
they clean up so nice
and I wish I could wrap up
the backwoods melancholy
in bow ties, in jeweled spiderwebs-
But it's too late.
The moment is passing,
it's glitching,
and I hope she knows
no matter the whats
the whys
in all this "how?"
my soul beats alongside
I river-smile when she smiles
even when the mask
turns this art of happiness
abstract
Joan Miro's "Seated Woman"
and I feel like oil shaped on paper
imagination floating
fantastically behind-the-scenes

cubed by my MacBook Air
as she's sipping champagne
practicing the waltz of her bridal voice
off in Nashville.

But I've learned that even the madness
of missing moments
sandwiched with the ones we've known
all our lives
and the fairy dust days
five-years-old to this sense of now
even as now flutters in flux
the insomniac nights playing pizzicato
the foreign moments of tearful distance
like a cassette tape unwound
ends hanging out
with songs still left to sing
almost larks in feathered joy
balancing cloud marbles
on beauty beaks
there's a force *fantastical*
in all that madness and distance
in all this missing
even in the glitching.

I know there's a spiderweb ally
and for a Babylon alphabet moment
I look no further
than how he lays the sincere
peanut butter on jelly
speaking pulsed whale call
magnetizing hawk's soar, sky to paper

THE ONES THAT MADE THEIR MARK

memorizing stone conversation
up to the Big Dipper
right down again to
moon pouring into the sea
turning it blue cereal
who hears the gold
that paints the lonely bright
that neon-connects us all
no matter how the internet
gets cold feet for minutes at a time-
And I wonder if long before
the world as I knew it
took a terrified breath
full of regret
of longing
belonging
stuck to time's bumblebee tongue
if Moses felt unpeopled
as his shocked corneas
paid mind
rapt to the sway
of atomic sandstone angels
and ferocious guardianship
talking in pure madness marvelous frenzy
heirloom china tea set exploding stars
something exquisite from the breaking
the changing
chugalugging
civilization's black holes
voltage-bathing the bush as he knew it
like human thoughts
hallowed in godly tuxedos.

In the emotional tundra,
people-close in words felt real
transforming
refreshing glow
spanning upside down quarantine distance,
Lee taught me to see spiders
fire-brave like Moses.
And in coming face to face
with honor
clear-eyed for miles in the net,
I felt seen too.

It's only now
I'm able to recognize
the force of middle-most
sidewise
time's turning point
like blessed ticks on a clock's
maskless countenance
that the universe pulled matter
friends and winds and poets
to stir alphabet soup
and find the lost art
of light and dark rallying
while the world we knew
remembered how to dolphin dream
again
anew
real and imagined
unsticking from the cobwebs
in lonely bright.

AQUAMARINE ABLAZE

(FOR MY TWIN)

Your breakthrough eyes dream up
aquamarine ablaze-
Moonbeams hanging on to
infinity whole.

Humans look up at the night sky
think it's effortless
to cast such phosphorescent light
but you know it's not
it takes eyes learning to catch
aquamarine ablaze
it takes prayers that feel
sometimes like they boomerang
around other wishes
sent through the black gold sky
your eyes closing
the River Seine running circles.

What snow-crystaled awe
to find the next morning
there's courage left
to blink aquamarine.

So often this is what I picture
when I think of how
determination *looks*
it catches and blazes
a scientist like you
canvassing DNA
coming home Friday at midnight
going after cancer cells in tiny dishes
all the while
passersby don't hear
your heart's tempo
it loves so big
it spins left-field
high as Olympic Games
hammering in merry-go-rounds.

I've seen it
on a Tuesday
wearing lab goggles
white coat pressed
pockets of resilience
how your mind kindles
launching leaps and bounds
like a cherry bomb sparking
thoughts dawning fire flowers.

We so often fixate on Excalibur

THE ONES THAT MADE THEIR MARK

we don't notice the precious stone
King Arthur pulls the sword
but what's incredible is how he draws it
there's courage left
to blink aquamarine
to try where others couldn't
to try when sometimes
impossible can feel rigid
as a sword caught up in stone
but you're cut from husky breath
winner takes all and best shots
cast-iron as a knight's legend;
you're the warrior
the woman who can draw it
make us forget the stone
tenacity like the sword's dynasty
you point it like a scepter
enchanted
Excalibur whizzing out of boulder
I see the gymnast artistry it takes.

You move your soul in ribbons
like an inspired paintbrush
with nothing to lose
so you use every color.
When you're seasoned
you have in hand
the poise of
you've-got-what-it-takes
outside looking in
they don't feel the bristled years
you poured into finding

calm in the tessellated chaos.

You want your daring to gloss over
invisible-
but still I catch
how there's courage left
to blink aquamarine
heart ticking levitated.
Life turns trapeze, and you run it
on your toes.

I want to sing witness
tell the scientists, the doctors,
the non-believers
'Watch how she eclipses!
Hear how
she makes stone release steel.'
You take to the air
like it's nothing
like you could run life's trapeze
breathless
aquamarine blazing
eagle-eyed.

So many just see the sword
but I know the slab of that stone
I know how it clenches hearts
like trusty blades
and I don't take my eyes off
how maddening rock divides
just watching you conquer.

AN ODE TO THE OPTIMISTS

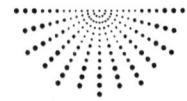

Spirit rises in secret
suns up tomorrow- I feel it.
A golden alto,
romantic as ever
in this daydreamer heart.

Sometimes a splash
in Thermos flasks
worn in milky mustaches;
frothed up above my lips:
clink, cheers.
My favorite brand of champagne flute,
bottoms-up bright side
moments of marmalade courage,
sweet and delicate
any optimist's true breakfast in bed.

Through rose-colored glasses,

the day still
steals through my window,
taking the edge off
soft and unafraid.
I bat my eyelashes,
letting dawn shine
dance between them.

COFFEE IN MY CLOUDS

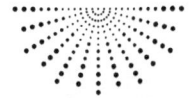

Today I splashed a cloud of milk
into my cup of cinnamon coffee
where three java hands
reached right out
weathering my white blouse
and I wondered if coffee were
the color of tumbleweed
and steaming mangos
well what a flattened sight
I'd make
all because there was a cloud of milk
a downpour in my second cup
all because three java hands
shook up my soft cotton
the one that dips in like a V
just how sometimes
my thoughts dart in clouds
chasing V shapes.

Well that's just *peachy*, I thought
how a V train of coffee stains
leads to cotton
brewing a French press
in the most unconventional way
and I waved my hands up
in a caffeinated temper
feeling like my day had been riding
on this shirt sailing through
feeling like there's an unspoken rule
when wearing a white dress shirt
it will be tie-dyed by mid-afternoon
feeling like my day went Elvis
all shook up
one too many coffee stains
signing this Tuesday in autographs
swirled by a rocking teaspoon.

Still, if a day floats as a shirt
and the coffee stains multiply
like tumbleweeds coloring lily ponds
on a blousy blank canvas
are there
clouds reaching from my coffee
or is there coffee yodeling reservoirs
around clouds of cream
reaching
hands to mix hopes and dreams
like how tears dart like thoughts
running from V shapes
chasing cafe au lait truths
that flatten a sight like me

THE ONES THAT MADE THEIR MARK

just to weather a girl right up
swirled by tie-dye come and gone
and meanwhile so much stirring
do you see how it steams by unannounced?

How funny that a shirt can be
washed out
softness gentle in a pool of sink
because a day can't be erased
with soap on improvised cotton
even if I'd want that
honestly, it takes hands reaching
it takes thoughts and clouds
the ways we make our own V shapes
to really see the coffee in the clouds
the shirt's spaces still wide open
and not just the suds on stains
when a Tuesday's left stirring
tie-dyed canvases like me.

EXPLODING INTO A VORTEX OF CONSTELLATION DREAMS

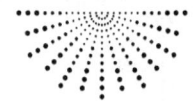

Thank you for filling
a sea with Northern Lights
to swim among mermaids of the stars
whose fins become streaks
painting the amethyst night
sky with blessed dust
songs humming from light
years before
curling time's
wrinkle of delight in a bend
that pulls us along with meteor tides
bursting with the richest
soul magic
bubbling through our eyes
singing in poet hearts
until the cosmic timing
becomes a matter of King Midas dust

dancing moon
dancing sun
dancing into the exploding dawn.

FOR RACHEL OVER THE RAINBOW

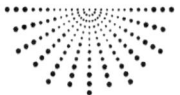

This weekend, I bought a used
light wooden-topped office desk
drawers to compartmentalize
and a copper key
to lock the top one
to slide what I might keep
close to my chest
away
as I ponder
what the person before me
shifted behind
into the waiting cube
a desk almost new
not quite- enough to have character
just like you'd appreciate
with sleek metal pewter legs
walking through
a slick mat made for

THE ONES THAT MADE THEIR MARK

ease of rolling
well-run
complete with something new
a leather chair
constructed for someone like me
to lean on
memory foam to
to try to memorize
if a La-Z-Boy chair
can really remember
the places I need
I want to be able to
lean on
just like that
label in large letters
'Big & Tall'
and I think of how you'd laugh
and how when you'd laugh
it sounded like you were singing
if yellow diamonds could talk
they might sound like you
and you'd say you were 'fun-sized'
I think of how you'd tell me
to leave this chair
in the time it would take to swivel
myself around
because I could lean on you
if ever I need
at Big Rock Park
where the leaves blush like heaven
dying to take angel colors
out of prayer drawers

gift them to park-walking humans
best of new friends sharing copper keys
beauty queens who don't know it
jewel shepherds of spirit
who are too busy watching the
angel colors bounce
to count the swivel-seconds
to that true mystery when
the when that takes by surprise
without a memo
without a season flush
their wings might
beam yellow diamond laughter
up to supernatural eternity
where I imagine desks
old and new
angels old and new and
missed missed missed on earth
can singsong laugh
and see rainbows in all that somewhere
spangle out from
delight-open ear-to-ear beams.

I think in ifs
if memory foam
in this new La-Z-Boy
another new item bought
without you to text me
to find out how it feels
to watch our giddy reflections
bounce how autumn used to
when you were here to share keys

THE ONES THAT MADE THEIR MARK

kinetic in salt-dusted margarita glasses
by the laughing Ohio River
because Kentucky seemed to share
in all our fun-sized jokes
I have key-twisting questions
if the cushion foam of memory
elegant and powerfully built
if it can fill in the spaces
where I'm missing missing missing
the angel spaces and colors where
I can't lean on you
the autumn margarita days
you didn't see from down here
the Big Four Bridge that they finally
brought to Louisville life.

The first time I walked
that bridge you
wish-prayed to see the day
when we could go together
to see the diamond colors
splash like margarita mix
into the vivid of a good night
I felt it didn't have
the richness
of your yellow diamonds joy
how not even new memory foam
is as legendary as an angel best friend
who I never dreamed would
slide past rainbow haze
before we could match
Cheesecake Factory cheesecakes

once more
who I wish I could scroll back
texts in time
take swivel-seconds out of the drawer
to say yes to every spontaneous
picnic invitation
every Hiko-A-Mon sushi deal at 6:30
devouring 2 rolls, 12 nigiri, easy
to share one more unlocked moment
a Batman movie marathon
a character I wouldn't know how to love
without you here to teach me
because you said 'the man bat'
had the superpower to be abundant
and I remember in the autumns
now colors blowing melancholy without you
how you were Batman-abundant
with the way your fun-sized love
and yellow diamonds
glow-shined in the hurt and lost spaces
otherwise locked
compartmentalized away
true-blue friendship like brand new foam
anyone could rest
their backs on
anyone who walked into the room
you with that yellow smiley-faced mug
backs you carried
heroine-effortless and
'fan-diddily-tastic!' divine
your genuine infinite
as heaven-sent rainbows

THE ONES THAT MADE THEIR MARK

laughing yellow diamonds
through lost clouds without
an autumn moon crescent
to turn to
through park and bridge hopes
and you'd want to have something more
than just a random green cardigan
for St. Patrick's Day
because every swivel-second was
worth the richest baked diamond colors
the right color green
that superhero nickname like 'Team Awesome'
or the sass of 'Team Not-So-Awesome'
the yellow umbrella you held like a
fun-sized sun
sunshine you'd bake along with purple icing
just for my surprise birthday cake
'I just want to be with you,' you'd say
happy for the company
for my company
and sinking into the foam of memories
I order sushi every time I can
I take greedy bites into ice cream sandwiches
even though none taste as homemade as yours
none are Batman-abundant.

I want to test out the used desk
that feels new to me
and it just seems that
everything feels oddly new
and somehow used
without you

a fractured feeling
that a new bridge
that a new chair
that new moments can still
take place
take some kind of walking
waking and sleeping space
new memories without you.

I want to take in
see if I can have
a pancake
in this La-Z-Boy chair
and I miss I miss I miss
the fun-sized
heart-wise insights
like your beloved Pancake Theory
how you'd make soul sense
if someone was the love of your life
if you could toss a pancake at him
and he wouldn't get stiff eyebrows
wouldn't catch seriousness like the flu
the last thing you'd want
is a temperament that couldn't
stretch cozy
someone who would struggle
to recline with softness
the anti-memory foam
no, the Pancake Theory
could learn a lover's wild
tap into a burst of inner treehouse
bubble-making play

THE ONES THAT MADE THEIR MARK

copper keys to joy
in colors like a mischievous
summer meadow
colors
twinned rainbow heartfelt,
peeking
like a carousel riding through a
popcorn-happening storm
colors like
splitting open dragon fruit
freshness
scooping out bright crimson
oh if this lover could laugh
and you'd laugh in yellow diamonds
the way you used to when
singsong sights for today's sore eyes
strolled parks on Kentucky earth
as this lover would toss the pancake
right back
syrup buttered-up love
angel soaring.

With memories of you
diamond foam stretches
and I can almost hear
bubbles and rainbows and laughter
turn even the smallest
fluffy buckwheat pancake
into a fun-sized adventure
something I hope
would make you proud
as I swivel in this new chair

that tries to support me
but can't be Batman-abundant
and I think that one day
I'll meet a new used heart
with memory foam feelings
who won't have met you
won't know the sound
of yellow diamonds laughter
won't know laughter can
shine deeper than autumn shimmer
and I'll toss a pancake
syrup buttered-up love
right at him
and wait for him to laugh
hope I can feel the coziness
of angels and rainbow haze
I never thought would swirl
in a great big carousel
fun-sized to pearly bridge hope
heights
and I'll be so so happy
for the blessed company.

WISDOM CAN TURN US TO CHICKEN

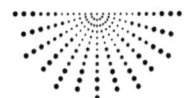

The lie tumbled far
children daring hands to stoves
they touch til it broils

APPARENTLY LUCY IS A DEMOCRAT

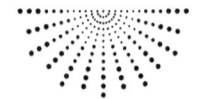

My neighbor shouts
with a broadcasted laugh
to his wife
as I pause and wait
for the two and their dogs
to stay or pass
as if he wants me to know
'*HA* apparently Lucy is a **Democrat**!!!!'
He looks at me
as if my choice to keep a distance
amidst a global pandemic
revealed me to be Lucy
and he wanted to
roll in the aisles over it
have a good ol' hoot and holler
right in Lucy's damn Democrat face.

THE ONES THAT MADE THEIR MARK

Now it's his turn to wait
to see if my facial expression
will stay or will it pass
will I blab my donkey alibi
through my Theraspecs sunglasses
make known in a way Lucy might
and I wonder what a Democrat would do
is this man that in an alternate universe
I might exchange a
downright-neighborly upturn head wobble
expecting me to sneer
is he expecting me to gasp
like I'm inhaling a
squirrel's latest fruit find
from a tree as tall as a beanstalk
that only leads to giant-sized trouble
for boys named Jack
is he wondering if I'll guffaw along too
join in the spitting nonsense
at that knee-slapper
at absurd Lucy's expense?

I feel my toes curl in my workout sneakers
remembering tomorrow is the day
to wear the new ones called 'Ghost'
but they're a half-size bigger
and I've grown kind of fond of
this toe-sized hole
a human-manufactured ghost
who walks with my steps
who can stand frozen for me

as I make up my mind
if this is a bizarre interaction
or if I'm living in an eccentric world
when a pandemic that leads us all
outside for neighborly walks more
brings a man like him to
lambaste this foolish Lucy
and to perform
for an unexpected audience
a girl wearing her grandmother's turquoise jacket
who can't help but wonder
if this is how it felt to be called 'Jew!'
when the Nazis took over
and neighbors would have laughed
uproariously
at the mere thought of one.

I ask myself if I'd ever brandish someone
Republican
when I know some on both sides
I have met some Republicans
who don't know what to be anymore
and I've met some stubborn Democrats
and none of them are just the one title
and don't we all poke holes
when our shoes get worn
do I carry political ghosts
that don't quite fit my curling toes?

And I walk by without so much as a word
liking that he'll never know

THE ONES THAT MADE THEIR MARK

I would drink a bourbon with Lucy
and I would have also given this neighbor
a bag of ice
without so much as a chortle.

WANDERLUST AT THE WISHING BRIDGE

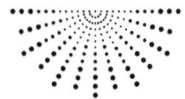

Who says I can't choose fantasy
like sugar wisps
unmeasured
by the glinting spoonful
swishing into a coffee mug
steaming with life?
I think I can love being mortal
as long as I can whistle sugar
even just sometimes
watch it sparkle mid-air
watch it crackle like
the wonder winds of travel
through my smiling teeth
that once had a mouth full of elastics
hooked to metal
top to bottom
the ways a taut bite can make a grin giddy
with the freedom of cuspids shifted

THE ONES THAT MADE THEIR MARK

because even what feels rigid can change
I feel the moving spirits of new lands
desert-warm against mouth pearls
toothy liberty whistling from old wires
the kind of breaths that bellow fantasy around me
that break in my new leather boots
the ones that say REAL LOVE.

Strong, sweet
just like the smoothie guy
makes my zippy smoothie
that magic stuff
where each smoothie guy
on side streets towering with fruit stands
says, *"yes yes, sababa, I know what you need!"*
and somehow it really is
what I didn't know I needed
Christmas Day through a Mediterranean straw
it feels that way when I've always loved
Auld Lang Syne
kindred fantasy
dancing that dusty kick of sunset cinnamon.

Cross my gypsy heart
full of honey wandering
full of spice love
horizon dreams and shooting star wings
washed clean with passing seafoam hymns
holding onto the Aquarius zodiac
these Kentucky hands touching mystic art
like the mosaic legend of this bridge
is flirting with my innermost desires

I feel them turn bursting mosaic —
Yes, I'm enchanted in the Promised Land.

Give me Jaffa, Jaffa, Jaffa
whole cream fairy-spun sugar clouds
teeth beam burrowing into whimsy
unforgettable over the Wishing Bridge.

DANCING WORDS

(FOR LP)

May the dancing words create
violins that sketch
versicolor chords
like feathers in the wind's
flowing hair
waving the wrinkle of time-
a captain's sail liberated
as the compass of the baritone
universe ticks
to the mysterious dance
insomniac with mighty song
pulpit in miraculous wave
a rataplan in misty voyage:
May the dancing words create
tangy equators
on the verge of believing
unthinkable worlds.

I FOUND MYSELF IN A REFLECTOR RED SEA

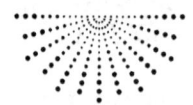

Right there-
I found myself in Eilat
late-20s free
as the palm trees coaxing
leafy skin to
disentangle sunset-swept clouds.

She sassy-smiled
with juicy ripe assurance
the kind that had
had its knots taken out.
I could feel it-
She just knew
when she chose to step back
not just out of habit
but to take a gollop
a rich breakfast of sea breeze;
when she wanted to let

THE ONES THAT MADE THEIR MARK

the Red Sea ruffle in a
horizon cheeks gust
heaven splash of dolphin-humming
like coral wiggling
endless light of day
spinning on mother earth's dreidel axis
through her hushed wild,
through her swing set curls.

There she was,
the *me* of my teen dream imagination
thin line tilting between
turquoise paradise and marvelous open sky,
and like the harmonica wind's melody
every translucent ghost
went off swimming,
droplets at last unblurred
Swayzes vanishing
see-through
into the gold-tinged blues
of a Red Sea
illuminated.
One by one,
they went diving
into the falling sun,
as I became ghosts-lighter,
gold-tinged blue taller,
life vest heart
full of paradise sea hopes
floating like hot air
into gingerbread tree fans.

I never felt so ghost-free,
so American-folksy alive
like the sunbeamy universe
took beautiful artisan fingers
dusty with clay-making
washing me blue-new
smack-dab in Camelot.
One of those impassioned reckonings
that take ginger-root down inside
where the life vest heart and ghosts of things
can get lost sometimes
but this turquoise time they opened up
solar wide as a magnificent desert howl;
inviting me
the me that I
finally,
years later
got the southernmost chance to greet.
That cactus-juice water,
dug sweet deep
beneath the sand left on knee faces-
rumbling ghost-gooey
dewy astir in the desert.

FEELING A WATERMELON SOLAR ECLIPSE

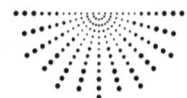

Today I learned
a wounded animal
lashes out
splintered
teeth bared
right into sunlit skin,
when souls get sunken in-
Capsized
as spooks bare
Hades hatchets;
When birthmarks feel
clotted, thick like
lemon rinds,
sour as citrus
peeled back with
a pocket knife.

I feel the phenomenon-

The solar eclipse of
your watermelon state of mind,
concealed to save itself
when shadowlands
turn up their old wedding veil.
Impossible to detect
to the naked heart,
but I always keep
a nightjar June bird when
the moon can just barely
make out a smile
through the mystic dusk.

My nightjar cries
1900 notes
in camouflage,
its small beak
seeking out
each vanishing minute
in flares of time.

That's how it hurts
between watermelon slicing-
A dehydrated cantaloupe
when we once spit out seeds
in sisterhood.

I store
your watermelon state of mind
for you
while you're leaving
starshine flesh bare and raw,

swallowing seeds;
lifting charcoal veils
as I watch you marry
your blues,
patient for you to divorce them.

I keep it hidden in the freezer.

HE WORE A HOODIE THAT SAID AUSCHWITZ

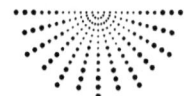

I think of Neny
she dyed her hair blonde
to escape death's camp

TEMPORARILY OUT OF ORDER

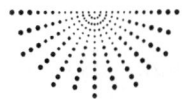

When life turns
tails over heads,
my strawberry heart bursts-
Bootleg optimism
hospital technicians chase as wild
geese; fluttering.

In some ways, I'm caught
in an existentialist play;
stage directions in italics,
hope stuck between parentheses.
Different Italian paintings on M.D. walls,
'the Italian experience' squared
neatly in a black frame.

Somehow these reception hallways all
show the same: the
waiting.

The floors are cherry wood.
I'm wearing glasses on glasses,
feeling meta and migraine diva.

My blood pressure skips quietly
around the cuff, a silver rush.
That's never the issue.

I'm a cool brain teaser- diagnoses chic.
EDM concert
full blast in chili pepper limbs.
Sriracha in tear ducts.

On a scale of 1 to 10, they never
ask me- how spicy does it feel?

I scribble numbers. I want
to point to a snow globe, shake it up,
and show you how
the glitter stays afloat.
Teach you how
I catch the light, like star mist
on my tongue.
Count aloud how
many times blue seas put the wind
back into my sails.

I wish you'd prescribe me
the North Star.
Skip light years,
waiting
rooms, those

THE ONES THAT MADE THEIR MARK

cursive 8s and 10s.

I want to tell you my legacy: let's go
beyond statistics.
Before I'm even born, my bloodline
hid in attics,
flew out of three-story
hotel windows, only an overcoat to
trampoline the fall.
My grandmother couldn't
pack her 17 year-old tenderness
in a folded suitcase
when she leapt.
She stowed away faith
in coat pockets.

Only a wise-too-fast teen,
Nelly Spitzer didn't turn
her sun-speckled back
on Bratislava
just to escape, to slip through
Nazi hellhound fingers.
She and Pablo took to
their heels
to hot air balloon
high past banshee numbers.
They freed themselves
from stripped-down digits
tattooing their flesh and blood.
They ran to cling to the land
of the living.

JULIE LAMB

I want to tell you when
my Neny first fled from
the vampire of lung cancer,
little Julie clasped her
wrinkled hands
covered in cream,
praying an old owl necklace
would bring us a
shelter of hope.
I want to put in my medical records:
My grandmother went on
to eat the richest cheesecake halves
outside of vampire clutches.
She flashed sapphire and pink coral
in her freedom eyes,
and she clung to the land of
the laughing, the Ecuadorian
orange cake-making,
the grandmothering.

I want you to see I grew up
to be Nelly's granddaughter,
safekeeping free hands and
thoroughbred horsepower
in well-worn coat pockets.

I want to scream against numbers
that have felt for eons
like cages:
You'll never catch me.

CALL ME PHOENIX

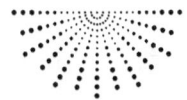

Maybe it's iridescent scar tissue-
In twine days gone by,
my best silks blow smoke
rings from 2018:
The year life bandied
a pair of gloves
at me,
and taught this
girl from Kentucky
how to box
like Cassius Clay
come 1963.
Before he was Muhammad Ali,
boxing up and down the aisles
of our family's jewelry store
telling my Grandpa Kenny:
"I'm gonna be the champ
one day, Mr. Lamb-

I'm gonna be the champ."

Rabbit punches ago,
caught me bare-knuckled.
Bloodstained upper cut
weeping
right
to my chin.
Going for the
amethyst
freedom from doubt KO.

I go for the right
cross
pouncing back in the ring,
learning to swing
just as I'm tracing
the elasticity in ropes
through corner posts-
It feels like the stretch
can go punch for punch,
40 years far in the desert.

I point my dangling finger
at the rusty scrape.

Try that again.
Let me see
the shadows bend
the veins in your gaze.

I confess

THE ONES THAT MADE THEIR MARK

I don't know rocket science- but
I've learned to play
jump rope with powder kegs.

I put my bouncy corkscrews up
in a buoyant bun- frizzing
Wonka elevator high.
And I train to one-two
right back.
Blush-colored
shoes skip up palm trees,
and sideways.

My footwork is never fancy.
But I'm a dark horse named 'Phoenix'
trotting on moonlit sands-

I pounce right up:
Float like amaranthine,
sting like a furnace-
Elbows bent,
leaping from cords,
praying hard as a mantis.

I hook bright as a prizefight
soft-hearted jewel
ripping elastic open.

EXTRACTION

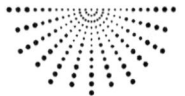

I've loved grasping pearls
wisdom cornered all those years
letting go pokes jaws

THRESHOLD NO. 5

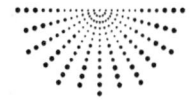

Empty waiting rooms
seem to lasso the same smell.

It's a feeling bottled up
like a stale Chanel No. 5
I don't want to wear.

Memory captures that distinct whiff
in perpetuity
that general sense of
I've been here before
it corkscrews through the nostrils
I feel it impatient on my tongue
the taste of waiting
that even a face mask can't block.

The lights gleam like heaven's doorway
so fluorescent I feel my soul

under inspection.

I'm glad I'm trying to be brave
trying is the opening act
as I wait I also remember
I've been brave before too.

Anxiety rides like a loop de loop
in all this waiting
and yet there I feel it
courage like muscle memory
flexing through the perfume bottle
filling what blanches in fluorescent fear.

EPILOGUE TO 2018: I SEE IN GOSPEL TRUTH

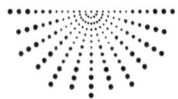

'3...2...1... Happy New Year!'

When the 2017 ball dropped,
I had left behind a brass mask.

But it didn't matter.
With Merlot-stained lips,
I kissed the old year
a sultry mocha goodbye.

My dress was leggy
serpentine flare
sweeping velvet
emerald green
when I held up my hands:
'Give me power,' I whispered
to the chandelier universe.

Three words I uttered-
and in 3...2...1,
a year of Hellenistic soul-sculpting
lifted off
invisible wood potter's ribs
set to shape me tall, inside-out
like unsmoothed clay
spinning edges on the wheel.

Israeli Neptune skies
opened like a fish mouth
to hoist my invitation:
'Welcome to your Thunderdome.'

If I told you what I battled-
Would you believe me?
How much could you
hold onto
with sparkler scars
of human touch
learning what the boss' hand feels like
knowing how he leers
ignored like rising stocks
behind closed think tank doors?
If you've never felt the wrath
of chronic pain's World War III,
would you dismiss
the bogeyman's return
bloodcurdling
surprise from under the bed
as hearsay lost in the dark?

THE ONES THAT MADE THEIR MARK

Parts of my year sound
science fiction.
The neurologist told me
it was as if my entire
sympathetic nervous system
railed civil war on my body
in a frantic
caterwauling
Led Zeppelin kind of flare:
A war that can only be won
gripping the nucleus of hope
in an airtight mind.
Some you can read about in
glossy mag toner, bold.
It's sad that those stories
have stopped surprising me.
The ones where I clap
for the female moguls
who dared
to call out the bogeymen
in a gutsy pyre of nightlight.

But here's what I wrested
from the baptism of fire:
This reservoir heart
winks within me
an eye in unhinged storms
blowing at two-by-two tigers
growling in stripes from Noah's ark
until the rainbow beckons
a shielded promise

I can almost hold onto
hues and thunder-tousled gleam
rock-ribbed
keeper of fire-eating faith.
I make out meridian-stirs
a balm of solstice
sunlight wedged
home free
high in the bell tower.

I now know that a picture is worth
a thousand
chambered words:
Like the one he captioned
"I redesign your dress" half-off
like the one where he photoshopped
my beaming face
on the Belgian intern's body
that confusing summer
I went home to Kentucky
to reunite with my family.
The pictures that got me transferred
away
from him to marketing,
a whole department
and yet the shortest footsteps
never fully out of reach
until at last
hitting "eject"
enough
just as I tend to

unencumbered sand
gentle beneath my wiggling toes
amethyst wool clouds fly
a gaping sunset covenant
how it claps and holy sings
head and shoulders above any storm-
mirrored back
in Middle Eastern multi-stories.

I know that I'm an ocean dragon
singing in bonfire tides.
I find the *how*.
Even when it's buried,
deep. I'll hypnotize
new nightmares- and they'll bow
at my crackling feet.
At every turn flashes
magenta Merapi sparks.

I dust off my glasses.
'Before you know it!'
I see in gospel truth:
nerve and
ceaseless starry eyes.

And the chandelier universe
whispered back,
'Look how she always comes ashore:
volcano-tall.'

I shake the Year of Power loose

like lava. It floats right off my mantle.
I form my own volcanic island.
My black pool of liquid sulfur glitters
by the steepest cliffs.

I rise in mountain swings from the sea floor.

ALLEGORY OF THE CAVE

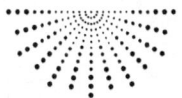

I glide in a shadow curtsy,
Queen of this cave of dark wonders-
I spread Cimmerian shade, like butter
on my knife.

It's my pueblo, and I'm a wandering star.

The doctors told me,
I can't see the reds, the oranges.
It's ok- When I close my eyes,
my brain swirls with a fizz and flush, of
unstoppable light.

It's as if my heart and mind, Collide.
It's as if hope has turned, Patchwork quilt.

But that's all a cave really needs.
A thing with feathers, stitched stone-blind.

It's soft and whispered.
But I make out a melody, of what-ifs,
just to hear Shadow Land whistle back:
'We won't keep you *por siempre*.'

The origin story goes like this:
Til I'm blue in the face, my brain glows-
like a scrambled sunset
whisking tangerine.
I open
my eyes. Asteroids land, dizzying
overhead.
My mom knocks on the cave,
a dove ruffling feathers,
"Come back to me-
come back from Mars."

And I'm somewhere in between-
Sifting through Plutos and lost moons.

Until morning breaks in prayer.
I wear my quilt
like a cape,
elegant and alive.

I always find my way back.

A WORLD INSIDE MY OWN DAMN HEAD

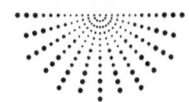

At the age of 30,
I found Samuel Taylor Coleridge,
Kubla Khan,
his sacred "vision in a dream."
I found him with an IV like a loose cannon
undulating magic Special K
into my purple-blue river arms.

I put up a "thou-shalt-not" order
when they try to ask me
about the charmed fountain, the fragments-
If they ever checker their way
in rebounding place;
into salmagundi.

"Why won't you tell us?"
They plead with me-
Because it's science of the mind.

We want to know what happens
to the daily dose of
anybody's guess.
What did the sick girl find
when she breathed hope
like dressed-up fog
onto the looking glass?

It's why Walt Disney conjured
a sleeping draught
for a dreaming beauty
jangling optimist's heart
aria to the worshiped woods,
magic bullet hidden
in a wise witch's spindle.

I keep these secrets asleep,
quiet as a mermaid queen
who traded her tonic song
for walking human legs.

Everyone's after the
catalyst tea leaves,
the eerie music of that
grass-and-lake-eyed
Pied Piper of Hamelin,
twinkling the notes for how
he bewitches a living band
under the careful watch of the sun.

How did Hansel and Gretel
ever make it out,

THE ONES THAT MADE THEIR MARK

woods-deep,
pebbles like questions
patient for a bubble of moon?

After all, Gretel had to hustle,
push that old witchy-woods woman
in a wolfish house of bread
wicked scorned fresh
baking a scarlet **howl**
Gehenna fire in the oven.

For a hesitating
tick of the clock,
the story could out-turn
Gretel-ciabatta,
and homemade Hansel cornbread
buttermilk to bony crisp.

But that's not how this story goes.

I pass on Lidocaine-
Let's keep this fairytale pure,
heartbeat fox thuds cheer up
the black monitor numbers tower
Ketamine dreams spinning
Rumpelstiltskin straw nerves
into Rapunzel up-in-a-citadel
witch doctor gold.

"Alexa, play Michael Buble,"
the magic pipe-
We're in Hamelin now,

and it's time to trick the fire rats
to leave my glass palace
under marvelous siege,
out the doors they overstayed.

It's me or the close-fisted witch-
Shaking with ice feet,
favorite bear blanket my cloak
I push her sunken face into the oven.
I don't know if she screams
or if that arm-twisting sound is me
grizzle-yowling:
"Get out of my house!"

I summon snow cloud powers:
All bets are off in this world
inside my own damn head.
No fable prepared me
as well as *A Wrinkle in Time*;
How I could call upon
safety, childhood bedroom shutters
bubbles for Rachel,
my best friend the peace angel
who went floating somewhere
rain wings
over a Noah's ark rainbow
sushi rice in the sky upstairs.
I bury blessings in what I call
Ketamine Land,
dandelions dance
ripple everywhere
for my nurse BethAnn.

THE ONES THAT MADE THEIR MARK

She glows hall light,
tells me they're
whisper-healers
undercover
golden Rapunzels.

No one told me how
war paint can look an awful lot
like rebuilding-
That I can get twisted
sweeping out my brain attic
as I jerry-build my body moat.
That whistling pain away like
Cinderella cinders
can make my eyes fill
moat millions,
from the princely silence.

No medical books would bet on me.
But I'm a wanderer,
a princess humming fairytales
healing flamingo
pouring jet ink memories
out the watery gates.
You can huff and puff-
Only neon turquoise
essential oil puffs circle
dandelions
blow petals down.

Here's what I'm afraid to
tell you,

and the woodland creatures
out loud.
Because you've never found
Kubla's Xanadu.
Because I'm shaking like a leaf
Snow White-scared
delicious apple-enchanted
that it's all a Pied Piper's dream.

Drinking from the well of restoration
feels like octopus luxury:
a kingdom of gorgeous *quiet*.

TIME'S SMILE WITH WRINKLES

(FOR LP)

You explode the melodies of blues
with bush-burning light
speaking into what secrets
make hearts heavy with purple darkness
tying ribbons of suns and stars
with wisdom of rainfall
that whispers seeds
urging them to dare
to lift their voices
through muddy soil
and find pouring gold
over fields
amidst the deep, dark wetness.

Time's smile with wrinkles
creates miracles
multitudes of wrinkles of wonder,
journeys

where space can be taught
to stand still
let souls stretch wild
take wind ears and hear
vibrato of light and rain and shadow
and full moon's mysterious, spectacular collision,
heartbeats thud-thudding with exuberance of listening
of *witnessing*, of testing toes mid-air
and jumping to the sky of eagles.

As our thoughts bubble and send tides
like seas majestic with frothy dreams
jumping like silver fins
our mind's eyes are
simultaneously leafy-wooded creeks,
courageous spiders with green dreams
spinning cobweb quilts around tree trunks
thick with wanting to be seen in the quiet
diamond-shaped mastery.

Somehow the first times
and re-awakenings dance like one
building on windswept harmonies
where rain plays harp to sun's
sweet soprano
where holy dark's icy bass
melts
the chords
fills silence with the lace fabric of intuition
all sung and heard before
yet notes finding symphony like glassy new.

THE ONES THAT MADE THEIR MARK

In creeks, in meadows, Neil Armstrong touching feet
to moon like clouds reaching for summer sun's bright
this is where the poets hum honest
and dancers twirl with reckless abandon
open to delicate intricacies
of this fierce wonder.

Let the moss curl around toes
in nature's
loyalty
let hearts
swim as we take our ears
deep enough we can hear
mermaids' twinkling echoes.

And bless the night
how it shapes light in ways
we never could have dreamed.

...LIKE I'M NO LONGER SCARED OF THE DARK

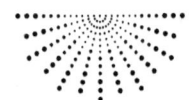

I love the Desert Beauty
butterfly rush:
Discovery
splashing up like
Niagara
high
past curiosity.

That first moment I realize
moss-green dinosaurs
wandered
long before we
became architects
building reading nooks
and alphabet nurseries
on forgotten pyramids
below bare feet.

THE ONES THAT MADE THEIR MARK

The first time a book
bigger than my
youngish eyes
taught me of Egyptian scribes
starving to remember,
to share buried temple secrets
against sandstone
cave walls.

Hieroglyphics:
the diaries that
painted sacred craters,
wisdom holy and in cursive.

I see a za'atar universe
in earthy puzzles.
I play jigsaw
with haloumi fossils
in the cafe;
I think I'm searching
through the eyes of
dynasties gone by.

What I find between
May Churchill Downs trumpets,
June melting guanabana ice cream
cones at the Mitad del Mundo,
and in Israeli winter, riding a camel
my friends and I call Moses the feminist:
Sassy J, in a looking glass.
Excavated in puzzle pieces, on street art-
spilled walls.

In 11 hour plane rides that serve
messy airport hair.
Through first kisses at Kuli Alma,
where nightlife reminds me of
sultry bourbon wrapping around
sweating ice cubes.
Spiritual witness to
how midnight Jaffa stones
yellow with ancient mysteries-
cast themselves into the new,
turning Tel Aviv hi-tech skyscraper tall
in the time it takes to stroll
by the unbroken sea:
Then there's me,
footsteps in the sand,
in the middle
of these modern-day hieroglyphs.
I fall in love as the
moon kisses the sun each dawn-
I never want to forget
the pretzel of old, new,
and seaside Middle Eastern
enchantment.

I realize I've never stopped
being a girl from Kentucky,
fried chicken sass and all.
Those gallops
still loud
as the Run for the Roses
in my footloose imagination;
Breathless.

THE ONES THAT MADE THEIR MARK

Standing from Banana Beach-
I shimmer
in around-the-world color;
Pictures on caves
exploding black-and-white,
bursting off walls.
But now: "bless your heart" with
Tel Aviv swagger.

This city is tough as a Tyrannosaurus,
carnivore teeth that can split
bashful bones in puzzle pieces-
Tel Aviv cooked
up the best parts of me,
straight to sizzle.
This city taught me to bite
through jawbone.

I wouldn't change
any of it.
Not even the cockroaches
Kafka might have dreamt
off the page.
They're slimiest in
corners.
I step over them now
as I walk through the Shuk,
skipping over trash.

I raise a glass.
Hit 'detonate,'
remembering dinosaurs

are not today's earth kings.
Let the liquor settle
in my veins. Gulp
fresh air
like a lioness learning
to roar.

Earn my growl. And let it
sing
through a storm of sea; let it
croon.

Bellow it 72 times over.
(*That's right- you heard me.*)

Clink the glass in
a royal empress 'cheers.'

This is how you make me feel, Tel Aviv.
Like I'm no longer scared of the dark.

SNAP, CRACKLE, POP: IT'S A PHOENIX KINGDOM NOW

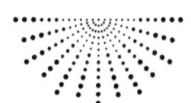

I now know how to snap, crackle,
and pop out of tombs
cockroaches thought they'd
build for me.
I'm a Kentucky-struck phoenix.
With only the sun on my back,
I watch the roaches roll off.

It's not their kingdom anymore.

You'll hear
my gallops and
dinosaur roars echo,
saving lions and birds.
They don't yet know
how to bite through bone.
I cast a sacred spell.

And I discover once more.
I step
into my new
Niagara voice.
My Desert Butterfly wings fly
high. The impossible sky is boundless.
I ink my name
in curlicues
in mystery clouds.

I love how it sounds.

ABOUT THE AUTHOR

Julie Lamb is a poet, globetrotter enthusiast, and sweet tooth explorer. Her appetite for life first sparked when she spent her childhood summers in Quito, Ecuador, eating poppyseed cakes in her grandmother's wooden house. In the spirit of the intrepid female travelers that came before her, Julie followed her love of food to Tel Aviv, Israel, where she spent over three years writing about the world, from finance to technology.

Before she leapt to the Middle East, she graduated from the University of Louisville with a Bachelor of Arts in English, all while taking every creative writing class she could (eating up words for breakfast like Gregory the goat). Her short story about a feisty parrot bumped its beak into the *Anthology of Short Stories by Young Americans*, and a sassy poem (based on Shakespeare's *Twelfth Night* with a modern twist) can be found bold as Malvolio in *The Lumberyard*. Julie Lamb's first play in high school, *Vexing Affections*, was a winner of Actors Theatre's Humana Festival of New American Plays, performed at Actors Theatre.

Today, Julie spins content magic at a colorful marketing agency in Louisville, Kentucky. This is Julie Lamb's first collection of poetry: a lifelong dream you now hold in your hands. She hopes you eat up every word!

www.ingramcontent.com/pod-product-compliance
Lightning Source LLC
Chambersburg PA
CBHW071258110426
42743CB00042B/1090